P9-BXY-965

GETTING OUT

BY **MARSHA NORMAN**

DRAMATISTS
PLAY SERVICE
INC.

GETTING OUT

Copyright © 1978, 1979, Marsha Norman

All Rights Reserved

CAUTION: Professionals and amateurs are hereby warned that performance of GETTING OUT is subject to payment of a royalty. It is fully protected under the copyright laws of the United States of America, and of all countries covered by the International Copyright Union (including the Dominion of Canada and the rest of the British Commonwealth), and of all countries covered by the Pan-American Copyright Convention, the Universal Copyright Convention, the Berne Convention, and of all countries with which the United States has reciprocal copyright relations. All rights, including without limitation professional/amateur stage rights, motion picture, recitation, lecturing, public reading, radio broadcasting, television, video or sound recording, all other forms of mechanical, electronic and digital reproduction, transmission and distribution, such as CD, DVD, the Internet, private and file-sharing networks, information storage and retrieval systems, photocopying, and the rights of translation into foreign languages are strictly reserved. Particular emphasis is placed upon the matter of readings, permission for which must be secured from the Author's agent in writing.

The English language stock and amateur stage performance rights in the United States, its territories, possessions and Canada for GETTING OUT are controlled exclusively by DRAMATISTS PLAY SERVICE, INC., 440 Park Avenue South, New York, NY 10016. No professional or nonprofessional performance of the Play may be given without obtaining in advance the written permission of DRAMATISTS PLAY SERVICE, INC., and paying the requisite fee.

Inquiries concerning all other rights should be addressed to Creative Artists Agency, 405 Lexington Avenue, 19th Floor, New York, NY 10174. Attn: Olivier Sultan.

SPECIAL NOTE

Anyone receiving permission to produce GETTING OUT is required to give credit to the Author as sole and exclusive Author of the Play on the title page of all programs distributed in connection with performances of the Play and in all instances in which the title of the Play appears, including printed or digital materials for advertising, publicizing or otherwise exploiting the Play and/or a production thereof. The name of the Author must appear on a separate line, in which no other name appears, immediately beneath the title and in size of type equal to 50% of the size of the largest, most prominent letter used for the title of the Play. No person, firm or entity may receive credit larger or more prominent than that accorded the Author. The following acknowledgments must appear on the title page of all programs distributed in connection with performances of the Play:

Originally produced by Actors Theatre of Louisville, Inc.,
in Louisville, Kentucky.

The West Coast Premiere of GETTING OUT was produced by
Center Theatre Group of Los Angeles, Mark Taper Forum,
Gordon Davidson, Artistic Director.

Originally Produced in New York by The Phoenix Theatre.

2

Produced Off-Broadway in New York City by
Lester Osterman, Lucille Lortel and Marc Howard.

SPECIAL NOTE ON SONGS AND RECORDINGS

Dramatists Play Service, Inc. neither holds the rights to nor grants permission to use any songs or recordings mentioned in the Play. Permission for performances of copyrighted songs, arrangements or recordings mentioned in this Play is not included in our license agreement. The permission of the copyright owner(s) must be obtained for any such use. For any songs and/or recordings mentioned in the Play, other songs, arrangements, or recordings may be substituted provided permission from the copyright owner(s) of such songs, arrangements or recordings is obtained; or songs, arrangements or recordings in the public domain may be substituted.

GETTING OUT was presented by Lester Osterman, Lucille Lortel and Marc Howard at the Theatre de Lys, in New York City, on May 15, 1979. It was directed by Jon Jory; the scenery and lighting were by James Tilton; the costumes were by Kurt Wilhelm; and the associate producers were Spencer H. Berlin and Marilyn R. Strauss. The cast, in order of appearance, was as follows:

ARLENE .... Susan Kingsley

ARLIE .... Pamela Reed

GUARD (1) (Evans) .... John C. Capodice

BENNIE .... Bob Burrus

GUARD (2) (Caldwell) .... Fritz Sperberg

DOCTOR .... William Jay

MOTHER .... Madeleine Thornton-Sherwood

SCHOOL PRINCIPAL ....Anna Minot

RONNIE .... Kevin Bacon

CARL .... Leo Burmester

WARDEN .... Hansford Rowe

RUBY .... Joan Pape

The play takes place in an apartment in a run-down
section of downtown Louisville.

The time is the present

World premiere at Actors Theatre of Louisville, Kentucky. The West Coast premiere of GETTING OUT was produced by the Center Theatre Group of Los Angeles, Mark Taper Forum. Original production in New York City by the Phoenix Theatre.

CAST:

ARLENE, a thin, drawn woman in her late twenties, who has just served an 8-year prison term for murder.

ARLIE, Arlene at various times earlier in her life.

BENNIE, an Alabama prison guard in his 50's.

EVANS, a prison guard

DOCTOR, a psychiatrist in a juvenile institution.

CALDWELL, a prison guard.

MOTHER, Arlene's mother.

SCHOOL PRINCIPAL

RONNIE, a teenager in a juvenile institution.

CARL, Arlene's former pimp and partner in various crimes, in his late 20's.

WARDEN, Superintendent of Pine Ridge Correctional Institute for Women.

RUBY, Arlene's upstairs neighbor, a cook in a diner, also an ex-con, in her late 30's.

Both acts are set in a dingy one-room apartment in a rundown section of downtown Louisville, Kentucky. There is a twin bed and one chair. There is a sink, an apartment-size combination stove and refrigerator, and a counter with cabinets above. Dirty curtains conceal the bars on the outside of the single window. There is one closet and a door to the bathroom. The door to the apartment opens into a hall.

A catwalk stretches above the apartment and a prison cell, Stage Right, connects to it by stairways. An apron Downstage and Stage Left completes the enclosure of the apartment in playing areas for the past. The apartment must seem imprisoned.

NOTES:

Arlie is the violent kid Arlene was until her last stretch in prison. She may walk through the apartment quite freely, but no one there will acknowledge her presence. Most of her scenes take place in the prison areas.

Arlie, in a sense, is Arlene's memory of herself, called up by fears, needs and even simple word cues. The memory haunts, attacks and warns. But mainly, the memory will not go away.

Arlie's life should be as vivid as Arlene's, if not as continuous. There must be hints in both physical type and gesture that Arlie and Arlene are the same person, though seen at different times in her life. They both speak with a country twang, but Arlene is suspicious and guarded, withdrawal is always a possibility. Arlie is unpredictable and incorrigible. The change seen in Arlie during the second act represents a movement toward the adult Arlene, but the transition should never be complete. Only in the final scene are they enjoyably aware of each other.

The life in the prison "surround" needs to convince without distracting. The guards do not belong to any specific institution, but rather, to all the places where Arlene has done time.

MARSHA NORMAN

OVER LOUDSPEAKER—BEFORE ACT I CURTAIN

These announcements will be broadcast beginning 5 minutes before the house lights come down for Act I. A woman's voice is preferred, a droning loud-speaker tone is essential.

Kitchen workers, all kitchen workers report immediately to the kitchen. Kitchen workers to the kitchen. The library will not be open today. Those scheduled for book check-out should remain in morning work assignments. Kitchen workers to the kitchen. No library hours today. Library hours resume tomorrow as usual. All kitchen workers to the kitchen.

Frances Mills, you have a visitor at the front gate. All residents and staff, all residents and staff . . . Do not, repeat, Do not, walk on the front lawn today or use the picnic tables on the front lawn during your break after lunch or dinner.

Your attention please. The exercise class for Dorm A residents has been cancelled. Mrs. Fischer should be back at work in another month. She thanks you for your cards and wants all her girls to know she had an 8 pound baby girl.

Doris Creech, see Mrs. Adams at the library before lunch. Frances Mills, you have a visitor at the front gate. The Women's Associates' picnic for the beauty school class has been postponed until Friday. As picnic lunches have already been prepared, any beauty school member who so wishes, may pick up a picnic lunch and eat it at her assigned lunch table during the regular lunch period.

Frances Mills, you have a visitor at the front gate. Doris Creech to see Mrs. Adams at the library before lunch. I'm sorry, that's Frankie Hill, you have a visitor at the front gate. Repeat, Frankie Hill, not Frances Mills, you have a visitor at the front gate.

GETTING OUT

ACT I

The warden's voice on tape is heard in the blackout.

WARDEN'S VOICE. The Alabama State Parole Board hereby grants parole to Holsclaw, Arlene, subject having served eight years at Pine Ridge Correctional Institute for the second degree murder of a cab driver in conjunction with a filling station robbery involving attempted kidnapping of attendant. Crime occurred during escape from Lakewood State Prison where subject Holsclaw was serving three years for forgery and prostitution. Extensive juvenile records from the state of Kentucky appended hereto. (*As Warden continues, light comes up on Arlene, walking around the cell, waiting to be picked up for the ride home. Arlie is visible, but just barely,* D.C. *Warden's voice, continuing.*) Subject now considered completely rehabilitated is returned to Kentucky under inter-state parole agreement in consideration of family residence and appropriate support personnel in the area. Subject will remain under the supervision of Kentucky parole officers for a period of five years. Prospects for successful integration into community rated good. Psychological evaluation, institutional history and health records attached in Appendix C, this document.

BENNIE'S VOICE. Arlie! (*Arlene leaves the cell, light comes up on Arlie, seated* D.C. *She tells this story rather simply. She enjoys it, but its horror is not lost on her. She may be doing some semi-absorbing activity such as painting her toenails.*)

ARLIE. So, there was this little kid, see, this creepy little fucker next door. Had glasses an somethin wrong with his foot. I don't know, seven, maybe. Anyhow, ever time his daddy went fishin, he'd bring this kid back some frogs. They built this little fence around em in the back yard like they was pets or somethin. An we'd try to go over an see em but he'd start screamin to his mother to come out an git rid of us. Real snotty like. So we got sick of him bein such a goody-goody an one night me an June snuck over there an put all

9

his dumb ol frogs in this sack. You never heared such a fuss. (*Makes croaking sounds.*) Slimy bastards, frogs. We was plannin to let em go all over the place, but when they started jumpin an all, we just figured they was askin for it. So, we taken em out front to the porch an we throwed em, one at a time, into the street. (*Laughs.*) Some of em hit cars goin by but most of em jus got squashed, you know, runned over? It was great, seein how far we could throw em, over back of our backs an under our legs an God, it was really fun watchin em fly through the air then SPLAT (*Claps hands.*) all over somebody's car window or somethin. Then the next day, we was waitin and this little kid comes out in his back yard lookin for his stupid frogs and he don't see any an he gets so crazy, cryin and everything. So me an June goes over an tells him we seen this big mess out in the street, an he goes out an sees all them frogs legs and bodies an shit all over the everwhere, an, man, it was so funny. We bout killed ourselves laughin. Then his mother come out and she wouldn't let him go out an pick up all the pieces, so he jus had to stand there watchin all the cars go by smush his little babies right into the street. I's gonna run out an git him a frog's head, but June yellin at me "Arlie, git over here fore some car slips on them frog guts an crashes into you." (*Pause.*) I never had so much fun in one day in my whole life. (*Arlie will remain seated as Arlene enters the apartment. It is late evening. Two sets of footsteps are heard coming up the stairs. Arlene opens the door and walks into the room. She stands still, surveying the littered apartment. Bennie is heard dragging a heavy trunk up the stairs. Bennie is wearing his guard uniform. He is a heavy man, but obviously used to physical work.*)

BENNIE. (*From outside.*) Arlie?

ARLENE. Arlene.

BENNIE. Arlene? (*Bringing the trunk just inside the door.*)

ARLENE. Leave it. I'll git it later.

BENNIE. Oh, now, let me bring it in for you. You ain't as strong as you was.

ARLENE. I ain't as mean as I was. I'm strong as ever. You go on now. (*Beginning to walk around the room.*)

ARLIE. (*Irritated, as though someone is calling her.*) Lay off! (*Gets up and walks past Bennie.*)

BENNIE. (*Scoots the trunk into the room a little further.*) Go on where, Arlie?

ARLENE. I don't know where. How'd I know where you'd be goin?

BENNIE. I can't go til I know you're gonna do all right.

ARLENE. Look, I'm gonna do all right. I done all right before Pine Ridge, an I done all right at Pine Ridge. An I'm gonna do all right here.

BENNIE. But you don't know nobody. I mean, nobody nice.

ARLENE. Lay off.

BENNIE. Nobody to take care of you.

ARLENE. (*Picking up old newspapers and other trash from the floor.*) I kin take care of myself. I been doin it long enough.

BENNIE. Sure you have, an you landed yourself in prison doin it, Arlie girl.

ARLENE. (*Wheels around, won't this guy ever shut up?*) Arlie girl landed herself in prison. Arlene is out, O.K.?

BENNIE. Hey, now, I know we said we wasn't gonna say nuthin about that, but I been lookin after you for a long time. I been watchin you eat your dinner for 8 years now. I got used to it, you know?

ARLENE. Well, you kin jus' git unused to it.

BENNIE. Then why'd you ask me to drive you all the way up here?

ARLENE. I didn't, now. That was all your big ideal.

BENNIE. And what were you gonna do? Ride the bus, pick up some soldier, git yourself in another mess of trouble?

ARLIE. (*Struts back into the apartment from the closet door, going over as if to a soldier sitting at a bar.*) O.K., who's gonna buy me a beer?

ARLENE. You oughta go by Fort Knox on your way home.

ARLIE. Fuckin soldiers, don't care where they get theirself drunk. (*Stops.*)

ARLENE. You'd like it.

ARLIE. Well, Arlie girl, take your pick.

ARLENE. They got tanks right out on the grass to look at.

ARLIE. (*Now appears to lean on a bar rail.*) You git that haircut today, honey?

BENNIE. I just didn't want you given your 20 dollars the warden gave you to the first pusher you come across. (*Arlie laughs.*)

ARLENE. That's what you think I been waitin for? (*A guard appears and motions for Arlie to follow him.*)

ARLIE. Yeah! I heard ya. (*The guard "escorts" Arlie to the cell and slams the door.*)

BENNIE. But God Almighty, I hate to think what you'd done to the first ol bugger tried to make you in that bus station. You got grit, Arlie girl. I gotta credit you for that.

ARLIE. (*From the cell, as she dumps a plate of food on the floor.*) Officer!

BENNIE. The screamin you'd do. Wake the dead.

ARLENE. Uh-huh.

BENNIE. An there ain't nobody can beat you for throwin plates. (*Proudly.*)

ARLIE. Are you gonna clean up this shit or do I have to sit here and look at it til I vomit? (*As the guard comes in to clean it up.*)

BENNIE. Listen, ever prison in Alabama's usin' plastic forks now on account of what you done.

ARLENE. You can quit talkin' just any time now.

ARLIE. Some life you got, fatso. Bringin me my dinner then wipin it off the walls. (*Laughs.*)

BENNIE. Some of them officers was pretty leery of you. Even the chaplain.

ARLENE. No he wasn't either.

BENNIE. Not me, though. You was just wild, that's all.

ARLENE. Animals is wild, not people. That's what he said.

ARLIE. (*Mocking.*) Good behavior, good behavior. Shit.

BENNIE. Now what could that four-eyes chaplain know about wild? (*Arlene looks up sharply.*) O.K. Not wild, then . . .

ARLIE. I kin git outta here anytime I want. (*Leaves the cell.*)

BENNIE. But you got grit, Arlie.

ARLENE. I have said for you to call me Arlene.

BENNIE. O.K. O.K.

ARLENE. Huh?

BENNIE. Don't git riled. You want me to call you Arlene, then Arlene it is. Yes Ma'am. Now, (*Slapping the trunk.*) where do you want this? (*No response.*) Arlene, I said, where do you want this trunk?

ARLENE. I don't care. (*Bennie starts to put it at the foot of the bed. Arlene sees him.*) No! (*Then calmer.*) I seen it there too long. (*Bennie is understandably irritated.*) Maybe over here. (*Points to a spot near the window.*) I could put a cloth on it and sit an look out the . . . (*She pulls the curtains apart, sees the bars on the window.*) What's these bars doin here?

BENNIE. (*Stops moving the trunk.*) I think they're to keep out burglars, you know. (*Sits on the trunk.*)

12

ARLENE. Yeah, I know.

ARLIE. (*Appearing on the catwalk, as if stopped during a break-in.*) We ain't breakin in, cop, we're just admirin this beautiful window.

ARLENE. I don't want them there. Pull them out.

BENNIE. You can't go tearin up the place, Arlene. Landlord wouldn't like it.

ARLIE. (*To the unseen policeman.*) Maybe I got a brick in my hand and maybe I don't.

BENNIE. Not one bit.

ARLIE. An I'm standin on this garbage can because I like to, all right?

ARLENE. I ain't gonna let no landlord tell me what to do. (*Fairly strong, walking back toward him.*)

BENNIE. The landlord owns the building. You gotta do what he says or he'll throw you out right on your pretty little behind. (*Gives her a familiar pat.*)

ARLENE. (*Slaps his hand away.*) You watch your mouth. I won't have no dirty talk.

ARLIE. Just shut the fuck up, cop! Go bust a wino or somethin. (*Returns to the cell.*)

ARLENE. Here, put the trunk over here. (*Points* D.R.)

BENNIE. What you got in here, anyhow? Rocks? Rocks from the rock pile? (*Carrying the trunk over to the spot she has picked.*)

ARLENE. That ain't funny.

BENNIE. Oh sweetie, I didn't mean nuthin by that.

ARLENE. And I ain't your sweetie.

BENNIE. We really did have us a rock pile, you know, at the old Men's Prison, yes we did. And those boys, time they did nine or ten years carryin' rocks around, they was pret-ty mean, I'm here to tell you. And strong? God.

ARLENE. Well, what did you expect? (*Beginning to unpack the trunk.*)

BENNIE. You're tellin' me. It was dumb, I kept tellin the warden that. They coulda killed us all, easy, any time, that outfit. Except, we did have the guns.

ARLENE. Uh-huh.

BENNIE. One old bastard sailed a throwin-rock at me one day, woulda took my eye out if I hadn't turned around just then. Still got the scar, see? (*Reaches up to the back of his head.*)

13

ARLENE. You shoot him?

BENNIE. Nope. Somebody else did. I forget who. Hey! (*Walking over to the window.*) These bars won't be so bad. Maybe you could get you some plants so's you don't even see them. Yeah, plants'd do it up just fine. Just fine.

ARLENE. (*Pulls a cheaply framed picture of Jesus out of the trunk.*) Chaplain give me this.

BENNIE. He got it for free, I bet.

ARLENE. Now, look here. That chaplain was good to me, so you can shut up about him.

BENNIE. Fine. Fine. (*Backing down.*)

ARLENE. Here. (*Handing him the picture.*) You might as well be useful 'fore you go.

BENNIE. Where you want it?

ARLENE. Don't matter.

BENNIE. Course it matters. Wouldn't want me puttin it inside the closet, would you? You gotta make decisions now, Arlene. Gotta decide things.

ARLENE. I don't care.

BENNIE. (*Insisting.*) Arlene.

ARLENE. There. (*Pointing to a prominent position on the apartment wall,* c.)

BENNIE. Yeah. Good place. See it first thing when you get up. (*Arlene lights a cigarette, as Arlie retrieves a hidden lighter from the toilet in the cell.*)

ARLIE. There's ways . . . gettin outta bars . . . (*Appears to light a fire in the cell, catching her blouse on fire too.*)

BENNIE. (*As Arlie is lighting the fire.*) This ol nail's pretty loose. I'll find something better to hang it with . . . somewhere or other . . .

ARLIE. (*Screams and the Doctor runs toward her, getting the attention of Evans, a guard who has been goofing off on the catwalk.*) Let me outta here! There's a fuckin fire in here! (*Doctor arrives at the cell, pats his pockets as if looking for the keys.*) Officer!

DOCTOR. Guard! (*Guard begins his run to the cell.*)

ARLIE. It's burnin me!

DOCTOR. Hurry!

GUARD-EVANS. I'm comin! I'm comin!

DOCTOR. What the hell were you . . .

GUARD-EVANS. Come on, come on. (*Fumbling for the right key.*)

DOCTOR. For Chrissake! (*Urgent. Guard gets the door open, they rush in. Doctor, wrestling Arlie to the ground, opens his bag.*) Lay still, dammit. (*Arlie collapses, Doctor may appear to give an injection.*) Ow! (*Grabbing his hand.*)

GUARD-EVANS. (*Lifting Arlie up to the bed.*) Get bit, Doc?

DOCTOR. You going to let her burn this place down before you start payin attention up there?

GUARD-EVANS. (*Walks to the toilet, feels under the rim.*) Uh-huh.

BENNIE. There, that what you had in mind?

ARLENE. Yeah, thanks.

GUARD-EVANS. She musta had them matches hid right here.

BENNIE. (*Who has hung the picture and is now staring at it.*) How you think he kept his beard trimmed all nice?

ARLENE. (*Preoccupied with unloading the trunk.*) Who?

BENNIE. (*Pointing to the picture.*) Jesus.

DOCTOR. (*Quite stern.*) I'll have to report you for this.

ARLENE. I don't know.

DOCTOR. That injection should hold her. I'll check back later. (*Leaves.*)

GUARD-EVANS. (*Walking over to the bed.*) Report me, my ass. We got cells don't have potties, Holsclaw. (*Begins to search her and the bed, handling her very roughly.*) So where is it now? Got it up your pookie, I bet. Oh, that'd be good. Doc comin back an me with my fingers up your . . . roll over . . . don't weigh hardly nuthin, do you, dollie?

BENNIE. Never seen him without a moustache either.

ARLENE. Huh?

BENNIE. The picture.

GUARD-EVANS. Aw now . . . (*Finding the lighter under the mattress.*) That wasn't hard at all. Don't you know bout hide an seek, Arlie, girl? Gonna hide somethin, hide it where it's fun to find it. (*Standing up, going to the door.*) Crazy fuckin someday-we-ain't-gonna-come-save-you bitch!

BENNIE. Well, Arlie girl, (*Guard slams cell door and leaves.*) That ol trunk's bout as empty as my belly.

ARLENE. You have been talkin bout your belly ever since we left this mornin.

BENNIE. You hungry? Them hotdogs we had give out around Nashville.

ARLENE. No. Not really.

BENNIE. You gotta eat, Arlene.

ARLENE. Says who?

BENNIE. (*Laughs, this is a familiar response.*) How bout I pick us up some chicken, give you time to clean yourself up. We'll have a nice little dinner, just the two of us.

ARLENE. I git sick if I eat this late. Besides, I'm tired.

BENNIE. You'll feel better soon's you git somethin on your stomach. Like I always said, "Can't plow less'n you feed the mule."

ARLENE. I ain't never heard you say that.

BENNIE. There's lots you don't know about me, Arlene. You been seein me ever day, but you ain't been payin attention. You'll get to like me now we're out.

ARLENE. You . . . was always out.

BENNIE. Yes sir, I'm gonna like bein retired. I kin tell already. An I can take care of you, like I been, only now . . .

ARLENE. (*Interrupting.*) You tol me you was jus takin a vacation.

BENNIE. I was gonna tell you.

ARLENE. You had some time off an nothin to do . . .

BENNIE. Figured you knew already.

ARLENE. You said you ain't never seen Kentucky like you always wanted to. Now you tell me you done quit at the prison? (*Increasingly angry.*)

BENNIE. They wouldn't let me drive you up here if I was still on the payroll, you know. Rules, against the rules. Coulda got me in big trouble doin that.

ARLENE. You ain't goin back to Pine Ridge?

BENNIE. Nope.

ARLENE. An you drove me all the way up here plannin to stay here?

BENNIE. I was thinkin on it.

ARLENE. Well what are you gonna do?

BENNIE. (*Not positive, just a possibility.*) Hardware.

ARLENE. Sell guns?

BENNIE. (*Laughs and shakes his head "no."*) Nails. Always wanted to. Some little store with bins and barrels full of nails and screws. Count em out. Put em in little sacks.

ARLENE. I don't need nobody hangin around remindin me where I been.

BENNIE. We had us a good time drivin up here, didn't we? You throwin that tomato outta the car . . . hit that No Litterin sign square in the middle. (*Grabs her arm as if to feel the muscle.*) Good arm you got.

ARLENE. (*Pulling away sharply.*) Don't you go grabbin me.

BENNIE. Listen, you take off them clothes and have yourself a nice hot bath. (*Heading for the bathroom.*) See, I'll start the water. And me, I'll go get us some chicken. (*Coming out of the bathroom.*) You like slaw or potato salad?

ARLENE. Don't matter.

BENNIE. (*Asking her to decide.*) Arlene . . .

ARLENE. Slaw.

BENNIE. One big bucket of slaw comin right up. An extra rolls. You have a nice bath, now, you hear? I'll take my time so's you don't have to hurry fixin yourself up.

ARLENE. I ain't gonna do no fixin.

BENNIE. (*A knowing smile.*) I know how you gals are when you get in the tub. You got any bubbles?

ARLENE. What?

BENNIE. Bubbles. You know, stuff to make bubbles with . . . bubble bath.

ARLENE. I thought you was goin.

BENNIE. Right. Right. Goin right now. (*Bennie leaves, locking the door behind him. He has left his hat on the bed. Arlene checks the stove and refrigerator, then goes into the bathroom when noted.*)

GUARD-CALDWELL. (*Opening the cell door, carrying a plastic dinner carton.*) Got your grub, girlie.

ARLIE. Get out!

GUARD-CALDWELL. Can't. Doc says you gotta take the sun today.

ARLIE. You take it! I ain't hungry. (*Guard and Arlie begin walk to the D. table area.*)

GUARD-CALDWELL. You gotta eat, Arlie.

ARLIE. Says who?

GUARD-CALDWELL. Says me. Says the Warden. Says the Department of Corrections. Brung you two rolls.

ARLIE. And you know what you can do with your . . .

GUARD-CALDWELL. Stuff em in your bra, why don't you?

ARLIE. Ain't you got somebody to go beat up somewhere?

GUARD-CALDWELL. Gotta see you get fattened up.

ARLIE. What do you care? (*Arlene goes into the bathroom.*)

GUARD-CALDWELL. Oh, we care all right. (*Setting the food down on the table.*) Got us a two-way mirror in the shower room. (*She looks up, hostile.*) And you don't know which one it is, do you? (*He forces her onto the seat.*) Yes Ma'am. Eat. (*Pointing to the food.*) We sure do care if you go gittin too skinny. (*Walks away, folding his arms and standing watching her, her anger building, despite her hunger.*) Yes Mam. We care a hog lickin lot.

ARLIE. Sons-a-bitches! (*Throws the whole carton at him. Mother's knock is heard on the apartment door.*)

MOTHER. Arlie? Arlie girl you in there? (*Arlene walks out of the bathroom, stands still, looking at the door. Arlie hears the knock at the same time and slips into the apartment and over to the bed, putting the pillow between her legs and holding the yellow teddy bear Arlene has unpacked. Knocking louder.*) Arlie?

ARLIE. (*Pulling herself up weakly on one elbow, speaking with the voice of a very young child.*) Mama? Mama? (*Arlene walks slowly toward the door.*)

MOTHER. (*Now pulling the doorknob from the outside, angry that the door is locked.*) Arlie? I know you're in there.

ARLIE. I can't git up, Mama. (*Hands between her legs.*) My legs is hurt.

MOTHER. What's takin you so long?

ARLENE. (*Smoothing out her dress.*) Yeah, I'm comin. (*Puts Bennie's hat out of sight under the bed.*) Hold on.

MOTHER. I brung you some stuff but I ain't gonna stand here all night. (*Arlene opens the door and stands back. Mother looks strong but badly worn. She is wearing her cab driver's uniform and is carrying a plastic laundry basket stuffed with cleaning fluids, towels, bug spray, etc.*)

ARLENE. I didn't know if you'd come.

MOTHER. Ain't I always?

ARLENE. How are you? (*Moves as if to hug her. Mother stands still, Arlene backs off.*)

MOTHER. Bout the same. (*Walking into the room.*)

ARLENE. I'm glad to see you.

MOTHER. (*Not looking at Arlene.*) You look tired.

ARLENE. It was a long drive.

MOTHER. (*Putting the laundry basket on the trunk.*) Didn't fatten you up none, I see. (*Walks around the room, looking the place over.*) You always was too skinny. (*Arlene straightens her clothes again.*) Shoulda beat you like your daddy said. Make you eat.

ARLIE. Nobody done this to me, Mama. (*Protesting, in pain.*) No! No!

MOTHER. He weren't a mean man, though, your daddy.

ARLIE. Was . . . (*Quickly.*) my bike. My bike hurt me. The seat bumped me.

MOTHER. You remember that black chewing gum he got you when you was sick?

ARLENE. I remember he beat up on you.

MOTHER. Yeah, (*Proudly.*) and he was real sorry a coupla times. (*Looking in the closet.*) Filthy dirty. Hey! (*Slamming the closet door, Arlene jumps at the noise.*) I brung you all kinda stuff. Just like Candy not leavin you nuthin. (*Walking back to the basket.*) Some kids I got.

ARLIE. (*Curling up into a ball.*) No, Mama, don't touch it. It'll git well. It git well before.

ARLENE. Where is Candy?

MOTHER. You got her place so what do you care? I got her outta my house so whatta I care? This'll be a good place for you.

ARLENE. (*Going to the window.*) Wish there was a yard, here.

MOTHER. (*Beginning to empty the basket.*) Nice things, see? Bet you ain't had no colored towels where you been.

ARLENE. No.

MOTHER. (*Putting some things away in cabinets.*) No place like home. Got that up on the kitchen wall now.

ARLIE. I don't want no tea, Mama.

ARLENE. Yeah?

MOTHER. (*Repeating Arlene's answers.*) No . . . yeah? . . . You forgit how to talk? I ain't gonna be here all that long. Least you can talk to me while I'm here.

ARLENE. You ever git that swing you wanted?

MOTHER. Dish towels, an see here? June sent along this teapot. You drink tea, Arlie?

ARLENE. No.

MOTHER. June's havin another baby. Don't know when to quit, that girl. Course, I ain't one to talk. (*Starting to pick up trash on the floors, etc.*)

19

ARLENE. Have you seen Joey?

ARLIE. I'm tellin you the truth.

MOTHER. An Ray . . .

ARLIE. (*Pleading.*) Daddy didn't do nuthin to me.

MOTHER. Ray ain't had a day of luck in his life.

ARLIE. Ask him. He saw me fall on my bike.

MOTHER. Least bein locked up now, he'll keep off June til the baby gits here.

ARLENE. Have you seen Joey?

MOTHER. Your daddy ain't doin' too good right now. Man's been dyin for ten years, to hear him tell it. You'd think he'd git tired of it an jus go ahead . . . pass on.

ARLENE Mother . . . (*Wanting an answer.*)

MOTHER. Yeah, I seen 'im. Bout two years ago. Got your stringy hair.

ARLENE. You got a picture?

MOTHER. You was right to give him up. Foster homes is good for some kids.

ARLIE. Where's my Joey-bear? Yellow Joey-bear? Mama?

ARLENE. How'd you see him?

MOTHER. I was down at Detention Center pickin up Pete. (*Beginning her serious cleaning now.*)

ARLENE. How is he? (*Less than interested.*)

MOTHER. I could be workin at the Detention Center I been there so much. All I gotta do's have somethin big goin on an I git a call to come after one of you. Can't jus have kids, no, gotta be pickin em up all over town.

ARLENE. You was just tellin me . . .

MOTHER. Pete is taller, that's all.

ARLENE. You was just tellin me how you saw Joey.

MOTHER. I'm comin back in the cab an I seen him waitin for the bus.

ARLENE. What'd he say?

MOTHER. Oh, I didn't stop. (*Arlene looks up quickly, hurt and angry.*) If the kid don't even know you, Arlie, he sure ain't gonna know who I am.

ARLENE. How come he couldn't stay at Shirley's?

MOTHER. Cause Shirley never was crazy about washin more diapers. She's the only smart kid I got. Anyway, social worker only put him there til she could find him a foster home.

ARLENE. But I coulda seen him.

MOTHER. Thatta been trouble, him bein in the family. Kid wouldn't have known who to listen to, Shirley or you.

ARLENE. But I'm his mother.

MOTHER. (*Interrupting.*) See, now you don't have to be worryin about him. No kids, no worryin.

ARLENE. He just had his birthday, you know.

ARLIE. Don't let daddy come in here, Mama. Just you an me. Mama?

ARLENE. When I git workin, I'll git a nice rug for this place. He could come live here with me.

MOTHER. Fat chance.

ARLENE. I done my time.

MOTHER. You never really got attached to him anyway.

ARLENE. How do you know that? (*Furious.*)

MOTHER. Now don't you go gettin het up. I'm tellin you . . .

ARLENE. But . . .

MOTHER. Kids need rules to go by an he'll get em over there.

ARLIE. No Daddy! I didn't tell her nuthin. I didn't! I didn't! (*Screaming, gets up from the bed, terrified.*)

MOTHER. Here, help me with these sheets. (*Hands Arlene the sheets from the laundry basket.*) Even got you a spread. Kinda goes with them curtains. (*Arlene is silent.*) You ain't thanked me, Arlie girl.

ARLENE. (*Going to the other side of the bed.*) They don't call me Arlie no more. It's Arlene now. (*Arlene and Mother make up the bed. Arlie jumps up, looks around and goes over to Mother's purse. She looks through it hurriedly and pulls out the wallet. She takes some money and runs D.L. where she is caught by a School Principal.*)

PRINCIPAL. Arlie? You're in an awfully big hurry for such a little girl. (*Brushes at Arlie's hair.*) That is you under all that hair, isn't it? (*Arlie resists this gesture.*) Now, you can watch where you're going.

ARLIE. Gotta git home.

PRINCIPAL. But school isn't over for another three hours. And there's peanut butter and chili today. (*As if this mattered.*)

ARLIE. Ain't hungry. (*Struggling free.*)

PRINCIPAL. (*Now sees Arlie's hands clenched behind her back.*)

21

What do we have in our hands, Arlie? (*Sticky sweet over suspicion.*)

ARLIE. Nuthin.

PRINCIPAL. Let me see your hands, Arlie. Open up your hands. (*Expecting the worse.*)

ARLIE. (*Bringing hands around in front, opening them, showing crumpled dollars.*) It's my money. I earned it.

PRINCIPAL. (*Taking the money.*) And how did we earn this money?

ARLIE. Doin things.

PRINCIPAL. What kind of things?

ARLIE. For my daddy.

PRINCIPAL. Well, we'll see about that. You'll have to come with me.

ARLIE. No. (*Resisting as Principal pulls her.*)

PRINCIPAL. Your mother was right after all. She said put you in a special school. (*Quickly.*) No, what she said was put you away somewhere and I said, No, she's too young, well I was wrong. I have four hundred other children to take care of here and what have I been doing? Breaking up your fights, talking to your truant officer and washing your writing off the bathroom wall. Well, I've had enough. You've made your choice. You *want* out of regular school and you're going to *get* out of regular school.

ARLIE. (*Becoming more violent.*) You can't make me go nowhere, bitch!

PRINCIPAL. (*Backing off in cold anger.*) I'm not making you go. You've earned it. You've worked hard for this, well, they're used to your type over there. They'll know exactly what to do with you. (*Principal stalks off, leaving Arlie alone.*)

MOTHER. (*Smoothing out the spread.*) Spread ain't new, but it don't look so bad. Think we got it right after we got you. No, I remember now. I was pregnant with you an been real sick the whole time. (*Arlene lights a cigarette, Mother takes one, Arlene retrieves the pack quickly.*) Your daddy brung me home this big bowl of chili an some jelly doughnuts. Some fare from the airport give him a big tip. Anyway, I'd been eatin peanut brittle all day, only thing that tasted any good. Then in he come with this chili an no sooner'n I got in bed I thrown up all over everwhere. Lucky I didn't throw you up, Arlie girl. Anyhow, that's how come us to get a new spread. This one here. (*Sits on the bed.*)

ARLENE. You drivin the cab any?

MOTHER. Any? Your daddy ain't drove it at all a long time now. 6 years, 7 maybe.

ARLENE. You meet anybody nice?

MOTHER. Not any more. Mostly drivin old ladies to get their shoes. Guess it got around the nursin homes I was reliable. (*Sounds funny to her.*) You remember that time I took you drivin with me that night after you been in a fight an that soldier bought us a beer? Shitty place, hole in the wall?

ARLENE. You made me wait in the car.

MOTHER. (*Standing up.*) Think I'd take a child of mine into a dump like that?

ARLENE. You went in.

MOTHER. Weren't no harm in it. (*Walking over for the bug spray.*) I didn't always look so bad, you know.

ARLENE. You was pretty.

MOTHER. (*Beginning to spray the floors.*) You could look better'n you do. Do somethin with your hair. I always thought if you'd looked better you wouldn't have got in so much trouble.

ARLENE. (*Pleased and curious.*) Joey got my hair?

MOTHER. And skinny.

ARLENE. I took some beauty school at Pine Ridge.

MOTHER. Yeah, a beautician?

ARLENE. I don't guess so.

MOTHER. Said you was gonna work.

ARLENE. They got a law here. Ex-cons can't get no license.

MOTHER. Shoulda stayed in Alabama, then. Worked there.

ARLENE. They got a law there, too.

MOTHER. Then why'd they give you the trainin?

ARLENE. I don't know.

MOTHER. Maybe they thought it'd straighten you out.

ARLENE. Yeah.

MOTHER. But you are gonna work, right? (*Doesn't want another burden.*)

ARLENE. Yeah. Cookin maybe. Somethin that pays good.

MOTHER. You? Cook? (*Laughs.*)

ARLENE. I could learn it.

MOTHER. Your daddy ain't never forgive you for that bologna sandwich. (*Arlene laughs a little, finally enjoying a memory.*) Oh, I wish I'd seen you spreadin' that Colgate on that bread. He'd have smelled that toothpaste if he hadn't been so sloshed. Little snotty-nosed kid tryin to kill her daddy with a bologna sandwich. An him bein so pleased when you brung it to him . . . (*Laughing.*)

ARLENE. (*No longer enjoying the memory.*) He beat me good.

MOTHER. Well, now, Arlie, you gotta admit you had it comin to you. (*Wiping tears from laughing.*)

ARLENE. I guess.

MOTHER. You got a broom?

ARLENE. No.

MOTHER. Well, I got one in the cab I brung just in case. I can't leave it here, but I'll sweep up fore I go. (*Walking toward the door.*) You jus rest til I git back. Won't find no work lookin the way you do. (*Mother leaves, Arlene finds some lipstick and a mirror in her purse, she makes an attempt to look better while Mother is gone.*)

ARLIE. (*Jumps up, as if talking to another kid.*) She is not skinny!

ARLENE. (*Looking at herself in the mirror.*) I guess I could . . .

ARLIE. And she don't have to git them stinky permanents. Her hair just comes outta her head curly.

ARLENE. Some lipstick.

ARLIE. (*Serious.*) She drives the cab to buy us stuff, cause we don't take no charity from nobody, cause we got money cause she earned it.

ARLENE. (*Closing the mirror, dejected, afraid Mother might be right.*) But you're too skinny and you got stringy hair. (*Sitting on the floor.*)

ARLIE. (*More angry.*) She drives at night cause people needs rides at night. People goin to see their friends that are sick, or people's cars broken down an they gotta get to work at the . . . nobody calls my Mama a whore!

MOTHER. (*Coming back in with the broom.*) If I'd known you were gonna sweep up with your butt, I wouldn't have got this broom. Get up! (*Sweeps at Arlene to get her to move.*)

ARLIE. You're gonna take that back or I'm gonna rip out all your ugly hair and stuff it down your ugly throat.

ARLENE. (*Tugging at her own hair.*) You still cut hair?

MOTHER. (*Noticing some spot on the floor.*) Gonna take a razor blade to get out this paint.

ARLENE. Nail polish.

ARLIE. Wanna know what I know about your Mama? She's dyin.

24

Somethin's eatin up her insides piece by piece, only she don't want you to know it.

MOTHER. (*Continuing to sweep.*) So, you're callin' yourself Arlene, now?

ARLENE. Yes.

MOTHER. Don't want your girlie name no more?

ARLENE. Somethin like that.

MOTHER. They call you Arlene in prison?

ARLENE. Not at first when I was bein hateful. Just my number then.

MOTHER. You always been hateful.

ARLENE. There was this chaplain, he called me Arlene from the first day he come to talk to me. Here, let me help you. (*Arlene reaches for the broom.*)

MOTHER. I'll do it.

ARLENE. You kin rest.

MOTHER. Since when? (*Arlene backs off, Mother sweeping harder now.*) I ain't hateful, how come I got so many hateful kids? Poor dumb as hell Pat, stealin them wigs, Candy screwin since day one, Pete cuttin up ol Mac down at the grocery, June sellin dope like it was Girl Scout cookies, and you . . . thank God I can't remember it all.

ARLENE. (*A very serious request.*) Maybe I could come out on Sunday for . . . you still make that pot roast?

MOTHER. (*Now sweeping over by the picture of Jesus.*) That your picture?

ARLENE. That chaplain give it to me.

MOTHER. The one give you your "new name."

ARLENE. Yes.

MOTHER. It's crooked. (*Doesn't straighten it.*)

ARLENE. I liked those potatoes with no skins. An that ketchup squirter we had, jus like in a real restaurant.

MOTHER. People that run them institutions now, they jus don't know how to teach kids right. Let em run around an get in more trouble. They should get you up at the crack of dawn an set you to scrubbin the floor. That's what kids need. Trainin. Hard work.

ARLENE. (*A clear request.*) I'll probably git my Sundays off.

MOTHER. Sunday . . . is my day to clean house now. (*Arlene gets the message, finally walks over to straighten the picture. Mother now feels a little bad about this rejection, stops sweeping*

25

for a moment.) I woulda wrote you but I didn't have nuthin to say. An no money to send, so what's the use?

ARLENE. I made out.

MOTHER. They pay you for workin?

ARLENE. Bout three dollars a month.

MOTHER. How'd you make it on three dollars a month? (*Answers her own question.*) You do some favors?

ARLENE. (*Sitting down in the chair under the picture, a somewhat smug look.*) You jus can't make it by yourself.

MOTHER. (*Pauses, suspicious, then contemptuous.*) You play, Arlie?

ARLENE. You don't know nuthin about that.

MOTHER. I hear things. Girls callin each other "mommy" an bringin things back from the canteen for their "husbands." Makes me sick. You got family, Arlie, what you want with that playin? Don't want nobody like that in my house.

ARLENE. You don't know what you're talkin about.

MOTHER. I still got two kids at home. Don't want no bad example. (*Not finishing the sweeping. Has all the dirt in one place, but doesn't get it up off the floor yet.*)

ARLENE. I could tell them some things.

MOTHER. Like about that cab driver. (*Vicious.*)

ARLENE. Look, that was a long time ago. I wanna work, now, make somethin of myself. I learned to knit. People'll buy nice sweaters. Make some extra money.

MOTHER. We sure could use it.

ARLENE. An then if I have money, maybe they'd let me take Joey to the fair, buy him hotdogs an talk to him. Make sure he ain't foolin around.

MOTHER. What makes you think he'd listen to you? Alice, across the street? Her sister took care her kids while she was at Lexington. You think they pay any attention to her now? Ashamed, that's what. One of em told me his mother done died. Gone to see a friend and died there.

ARLENE. Be different with me and Joey.

MOTHER. He don't even know who you are, Arlie.

ARLENE. Arlene. (*She can't respond, this is all she can say.*)

MOTHER. You forgot already what you was like as a kid. At Waverly, tellin them lies about that campin trip we took, sayin

26

your Daddy made you watch while he an me . . . you know. I'd have killed you then if them social workers hadn't been watchin.

ARLENE. Yeah.

MOTHER. Didn't want them thinkin I weren't fit. Well, what do they know? Each time you'd get out of one of them places, you'd be actin worse than ever. Go right back to that junkie, pimp, Carl, sellin the stuff he steals, savin his ass from the police. He follow you home this time, too?

ARLENE. He's got four more years at Bricktown.

MOTHER. Glad to hear it. Here . . . (*Handing her a bucket.*) Water. (*Arlene fills up the bucket and Mother washes several dirty spots on the walls, floor and furniture. Arlene knows better than to try to help. The Doctor walks D. to find Arlie for their counseling session.*)

DOCTOR. So you refuse to go to camp?

ARLIE. Now why'd I want to go to your fuckin camp? Camp's for babies. You can go shit in the woods if you want to, but I ain't goin.

DOCTOR. Oh, you're goin.

ARLIE. Wanna bet?

MOTHER. Arlie, I'm waitin. (*For the water.*)

ARLIE. 'Sides, I'm waitin.

DOCTOR. Waiting for what?

ARLIE. For Carl to come git me.

DOCTOR. And who is Carl?

ARLIE. Jus some guy. We're goin to Alabama.

DOCTOR. You don't go till we say you can go.

ARLIE. Carl's got a car.

DOCTOR. Does he have a driver's license to go with it?

ARLIE. (*Enraged, impatient.*) I'm goin now. (*She stalks away, then backs up toward him again. He has information she wants.*)

DOCTOR. Hey!

ARLENE. June picked out a name for the baby?

MOTHER. Clara . . . or Clarence. Got it from this fancy shampoo she bought.

ARLIE. I don't feel good. I'm pregnant, you know.

DOCTOR. The test was negative.

ARLIE. Well, I should know, shouldn't I?

DOCTOR. No. You want to be pregnant, is that it?

27

ARLIE. I wouldn't mind. Kids need somebody to bring em up right.

DOCTOR. Raising children is a big responsibility, you know.

ARLIE. Yeah, I know it. I ain't dumb. Everybody always thinks I'm so dumb.

DOCTOR. You could learn if you wanted to. That's what the teachers are here for.

ARLIE. Shit.

DOCTOR. Or so they say.

ARLIE. All they teach us is about geography. Why'd I need to know about Africa. Jungles and shit.

DOCTOR. They want you to know about other parts of the world.

ARLIE. Well, I ain't goin there so whatta I care?

DOCTOR. What's this about Cindy?

ARLIE. (*Hostile.*) She told Mr. Dawson some lies about me.

DOCTOR. I bet.

ARLIE. She said I fuck my Daddy for money.

DOCTOR. And what did you do when she said that?

ARLIE. What do you think I did? I beat the shit out of her.

DOCTOR. And that's a good way to work out your problem?

ARLIE. She ain't done it since. (*Proud.*)

DOCTOR. She's been in traction, since.

ARLIE. So, whatta I care? She say it again, I'll do it again. Bitch!

ARLENE. (*Looking down at the dirt Mother is gathering on the floor.*) I ain't got a can. Just leave it.

MOTHER. And have you sweep it under the bed after I go? (*Wraps the dirt in a piece of newspaper and puts it in her laundry basket.*)

DOCTOR. (*Looking at his clipboard.*) You're on unit clean-up this week.

ARLIE. I done it last week!

DOCTOR. Then you should remember what to do. The session is over. (*Getting up, walking away.*) And stand up straight! And take off that hat! (*Doctor and Arlie go offstage as Mother finds Bennie's hat.*)

MOTHER. This your hat?

ARLENE. No.

MOTHER. Guess Candy left it here.

ARLENE. Candy didn't leave nuthin. (*Then realizes this was a mistake.*)

MOTHER. Then whose is it? (*Arlene doesn't answer.*) Do you know whose hat this is? (*Arlene turns away.*) I'm askin you a question and I want an answer. (*Arlene turns her back to Mother.*) Whose hat is this? You tell me right now, whose hat is this?

ARLENE. It's Bennie's.

MOTHER. And who's Bennie?

ARLENE. Guy drove me home from Pine Ridge. A guard.

MOTHER. (*Upset.*) I knew it. You been screwin a goddamn guard. (*Throws the hat on the bed.*)

ARLENE. He jus drove me up here, that's all.

MOTHER. Sure.

ARLENE. I git sick on the bus.

MOTHER. You expect me to believe that?

ARLENE. I'm tellin you, he jus . . .

MOTHER. No man alive gonna drive a girl 500 miles for nuthin.

ARLENE. He ain't never seen Kentucky.

MOTHER. It ain't Kentucky he wants to see.

ARLENE. He ain't gettin nuthin from me.

MOTHER. That's what you think.

ARLENE. He done some nice things for me at Pine Ridge. Gum, funny stories.

MOTHER. He'd be tellin stories all right, tellin his buddies where to find you.

ARLENE. He's gettin us some dinner right now.

MOTHER. And how're you gonna pay him? Huh? Tell me that.

ARLENE. I ain't like that no more.

MOTHER. Oh you ain't. I'm your mother. I know what you'll do.

ARLENE. I tell you I ain't.

MOTHER. I knew it. Well, when you got another bastard in you, don't come cryin to me, cause I done told you.

ARLENE. Don't worry.

MOTHER. An I'm gettin myself outta here fore your boyfriend comes back.

ARLENE. He ain't my boyfriend. (*Increasing anger.*)

MOTHER. I been a lotta things, but I ain't dumb, Arlene. (*"Arlene" is mocking.*)

ARLENE. I didn't say you was. (*Beginning to know how this is going to turn out.*)

MOTHER. Oh no? You lied to me!

ARLENE. How?

MOTHER. You took my spread without even sayin thank you. (*Not an answer. Just going on with the fury.*) You're hintin at comin to my house for pot roast just like nuthin ever happened, an all the time you're hidin a goddamn guard under your bed. (*Furious.*) Uh-huh.

ARLENE. Mama? (*Quietly.*)

MOTHER. What? (*Cold, fierce.*)

ARLENE. What kind of meat makes a pot roast?

MOTHER. A roast makes a pot roast. Buy a roast. Shoulder, chuck . . .

ARLENE. Are you comin back?

MOTHER. You ain't got no need for me.

ARLENE. I gotta ask you to come see me?

MOTHER. I come tonight, didn't I, an nobody asked me?

ARLENE. Just forget it.

MOTHER. (*Getting her things together now, ready to go.*) An if I hadn't told them about this apartment, you wouldn't be out at all, how bout that!

ARLENE. Forget it! (*Stronger.*)

MOTHER. Don't you go talkin to me that way. You remember who I am. I'm the one took you back after all you done all them years. I brung you that teapot. I scrubbed your place. You remember that when you talk to me.

ARLENE. Sure.

MOTHER. Uh-huh. (*Now goes to the bed, rips off the spread and stuffs it in her basket.*) I knowed I shouldn't have come. You ain't changed a bit.

ARLENE. Same hateful brat, right? (*Back to Mother.*)

MOTHER. Same hateful brat. Right. (*Arms full, heading for the door.*)

ARLENE. (*Rushing toward her.*) Mama . . .

MOTHER. Don't you touch me. (*Mother leaves. Arlene stares out the door, stunned and hurt, finally, she slams the door and turns back into the room.*)

ARLENE. No! Don't you touch Mama, Arlie.

RONNIE. (*A fellow juvenile offender, runs across the catwalk, waving a necklace and being chased by Arlie.*) Arlie got a boyfriend, Arlie got a boyfriend. (*Throws the necklace D.*) Whoo!

30

ARLIE. (*Chasing him.*) Ronnie, you ugly mother, I'll smash your fuckin . . .

ARLENE. You might steal all . . . (*Getting more angry.*)

RONNIE. (*Running down the stairs.*) Arlie got a boyfriend . . .

ARLIE. Gimme that necklace or I'll . . .

ARLENE. . . . or eat all Mama's precious pot roast . . .

RONNIE. (*As they wrestle on the D. apron.*) You'll tell the Doctor on me? And get your private room back? (*Laughing.*)

ARLENE. (*Cold and hostile.*) No, don't touch Mama, Arlie. Cause you might slit Mama's throat. (*Goes into the bathroom.*)

ARLIE. You wanna swallow all them dirty teeth?

RONNIE. Tell me who give it to you.

ARLIE. No, you tell me where it's at.

RONNIE. (*Breaks away, pushing Arlie in the opposite direction, runs for the necklace.*) It's right here. (*Drops it down his pants.*) Come an git it.

ARLIE. Oh now, that was really ignorant, you stupid pig.

RONNIE. (*Backing away, daring her.*) Jus reach right in. First come, first served.

ARLIE. Now, how you gonna pee after I throw your weenie over the fence?

RONNIE. You ain't gonna do that, girl. You gonna fall in love. (*She turns vicious, pins him down, attacking. This is no longer play. He screams. Doctor appears on the catwalk.*)

DOCTOR. Arlie! (*Heads down the stairs to stop this.*)

CARL. (*From outside the apartment door.*) Arlie!

DOCTOR. Arlie!

ARLIE. Stupid, ugly . . .

RONNIE. Help! (*Arlie runs off, hides D.L.*)

DOCTOR. That's three more weeks of isolation, Arlie. (*Bending down to Ronnie.*) You all right? Can you walk?

RONNIE. (*Looking back to Arlie as he gets up in great pain.*) She was tryin to kill me.

DOCTOR. Yeah. Easy now. You shouldn've known, Ronnie.

ARLIE. (*Yelling at Ronnie.*) You'll get yours, crybaby.

CARL. Arlie . . .

ARLIE. Yeah, I'm comin!

CARL. Bad-lookin dude says move your ass an open up this here door, girl. (*Arlene does not come out of the bathroom. Carl twists the door knob violently, then kicks in the door and walks in. Carl is thin and cheaply dressed. Carl's walk and manner are imitative of black pimps, but he can't quite carry it off.*) Where you at, Mama?

ARLENE. Carl?

CARL. Who else? You 'spectin' Leroy Brown?

ARLENE. I'm takin a bath!

CARL. (*Walking toward the bathroom.*) I like my ladies clean. Matter of professional pride.

ARLENE. Don't come in here.

CARL. (*Mocking her tone.*) Don't come in here. I seen it all before, girl.

ARLENE. I'm gittin out. Sit down or somethin.

CARL. (*Talking loud enough for her to hear him through the door.*) Ain't got the time. (*Opens her purse, then searches the trunk.*) Jus come by to tell you it's tomorrow. We be takin our feet to the New York street. (*As though she will be pleased.*) No more fuckin around with these jiveass southern turkeys. We're goin to the big city, baby. Get you some red shades and some red shorts an the john's be linin' up fore we hit town. Four tricks a night. How's that sound? No use wearin out that cute ass you got. Way I hear it, only way to git busted up there's be stupid, an I ain't lived this long bein stupid.

ARLENE. (*Coming out of the bathroom wearing a towel.*) That's exactly how you lived your whole life—bein stupid.

CARL. Arlie . . . (*Moving in on her.*) be sweet, sugar.

ARLENE. Still got your curls.

CARL. (*Trying to hug her.*) You're lookin O.K. yourself.

ARLENE. Oh, Carl. (*Noticing the damage to the door, breaking away from any closeness he might try to force.*)

CARL. (*Amused.*) Bent up your door, some.

ARLENE. How come you're out?

CARL. Sweetheart, you done broke out once, been nabbed and sent to Pine Ridge and got yourself paroled since I been in. I got a right to a little free time too, ain't that right?

ARLENE. You escape?

CARL. Am I standin here or am I standin here? They been fuckin with you, I can tell.

ARLENE. They gonna catch you.

CARL. (*Going to the window.*) Not where we're going. Not a chance.

ARLENE. Where you goin they won't git you?

CARL. Remember that green hat you picked out for me down in Birmingham? Well, I ain't ever wore it yet, but I kin wear it in New York cause New York's where you wear whatever you feel like. One guy tol me he saw this dude wearin a whole ring of feathers roun his leg, right here (*Grabs his leg above the knee.*) an he weren't in no circus nor no Indian neither.

ARLENE. I ain't seen you since Birmingham. How come you think I wanna see you now?

ARLIE. (*Appearing suddenly, confronts Carl.*) Carl, I ain't goin with that dude, he's weird. (*Pointing as if there is a trick waiting.*)

CARL. Cause we gotta go collect the johns' money, that's "how come."

ARLIE. I don't need you pimpin for me.

ARLENE. (*Very strong.*) I'm gonna work.

CARL. Work?

ARLENE. Yeah.

CARL. What's this "work"?

ARLIE. You always sendin me to them ol' droolers . . .

CARL. You kin do two things, girl . . .

ARLIE. They slobberin all over me . . .

CARL. Breakin out an hookin.

ARLIE. They tyin me to the bed!

ARLENE. I mean real work.

ARLIE. (*Now screaming, gets further away from him.*) I could git killed working for you. Some sicko, some crazy drunk . . . (*Goes offstage, guard puts her in the cell sometime before Bennie's entrance.*)

CARL. You furget, we seen it all on TV in the dayroom, you bustin outta Lakewood like that. Fakin that palsy fit, then beatin that guard half to death with his own key ring. Whoo-ee! Then that spree you went on . . . stoppin at that fillin station for some cash, then kidnappin the old dude pumpin the gas.

ARLENE. Yeah.

CARL. Then that cab driver comes outta the bathroom an tries to mess with you and you shoots him with his own piece. (*Fires an imaginary pistol.*) That there's nice work, Mama. (*Going over to her, putting his arms around her.*)

ARLENE. That gun . . . it went off, Carl.

33

CARL. (*Getting more determined with his affection.*) That's what guns do, doll. They go off.

BENNIE'S VOICE. (*From outside.*) Arlene? Arlene?

CARL. Arlene? (*Jumping up.*) Well, la de da. (*Bennie opens the door, carrying the chicken dinners. He is confused seeing Arlene wearing a towel and talking to Carl.*)

ARLENE. Bennie, this here's Carl.

CARL. You're interruptin, Jack. Me an Arlie got business.

BENNIE. She's callin herself Arlene.

CARL. I call my ladies what I feel like, chicken man, an you call yourself "gone."

BENNIE. I don't take orders from you.

CARL. Well, you been takin orders from somebody, or did you git that outfit at the army surplus store?

ARLENE. Bennie brung me home from Pine Ridge.

CARL. (*Walking toward him.*) Oh, it's a guard now, is it? That chicken break out or what? (*Grabs the chicken.*)

BENNIE. I don't know what you're doin here, but . . .

CARL. What you gonna do about it, huh? Lock me up in the toilet? You an who else, Batman?

BENNIE. (*Taking the chicken back, walking calmly to the counter.*) Watch your mouth, punk. (*Condescending. Doesn't want a fight, for Arlene's sake, but doesn't want to appear threatened either.*)

CARL. (*Kicks a chair toward Bennie.*) Punk!

ARLENE. (*Trying to stop this.*) I'm hungry.

BENNIE. You heard her, she's hungry.

CARL. (*Vicious*). Shut up! (*Mocking.*) Ossifer.

BENNIE. Arlene, tell this guy if he knows what's good for him . . .

CARL (*Walking to the counter where Bennie has left the chicken.*) Why don't you write me a parkin ticket? (*Shoves the chicken on the floor.*) Don't fuck with me, Dad. It ain't healthy.

BENNIE. (*Pauses, a real standoff. Finally, bends down and picks up the chicken.*) You ain't worth dirtyin' my hands. (*Carl walks by him, laughing.*)

CARL. Hey, Arlie. I got some dude to see. (*For Bennie's benefit as he struts to the door.*) What I need with another beat up guard? All that blood, jus ugly up my threads. (*Very sarcastic.*) Bye y'all.

ARLENE. Bye, Carl.

CARL. (*Turns back quickly at the door, stopping Bennie who was following him.*) You really oughta shine them shoes, man. (*Vindictive laugh, slams the door in Bennie's face.*)

BENNIE. (*Relieved, trying to change the atmosphere.*) Well, how bout if we eat? You'll catch your death dressed like that.

ARLENE. Turn around then. (*Arlene gets a shabby housecoat from the closet. She puts it on over her towel, buttons it up, then pulls the towel out from under it. This has the look of a prison ritual.*)

BENNIE. (*As she is dressing.*) Your parole officer's gonna tell you to keep away from guys like that . . . for your own good, you know. Those types, just like the suckers on my tomatoes back home. Take everything right outta you. Gotta pull em off, Arlie, uh, Arlene.

ARLENE. Now, I'm decent now.

BENNIE. You hear what I said?

ARLENE. I told him that. That's exactly what I did tell him. (*Going to the bathroom for her hairbrush.*)

BENNIE. Who was that anyhow? (*Sits down on the bed, opens up the chicken.*)

ARLENE. (*From the bathroom.*) Long time ago, me an Carl took a trip together.

BENNIE. When you was a kid, you mean?

ARLENE. I was at this place for kids.

BENNIE. And Carl was there?

ARLENE. No, he picked me up an we went to Alabama. There was this wreck an all. I ended up at Lakewood for forgery. It was him that done it. Got me pregnant too.

BENNIE. That was Joey's father?

ARLENE. Yeah, but he don't know that. (*Sits down.*)

BENNIE. Just as well. Guy like that, don't know what they'd do.

ARLENE. Mother was here while ago. Says she's seen Joey. (*Taking a napkin from Bennie.*)

BENNIE. Wish I had a kid. Life ain't, well, complete, without no kids to play ball with an take fishin. Dorrie, though, she had them backaches an that neuralgia, day I married her to the day she died. Good woman though. No drinkin, no card playin, real sweet voice . . . what was that song she used to sing? . . . Oh, yeah . . .

ARLENE. She says Joey's a real good-lookin kid.

BENNIE. Well, his Mom ain't bad.

ARLENE. At Lakewood, they tried to git me to have an abortion.

35

BENNIE. They was just thinkin of you, Arlene.

ARLENE. I told em I'd kill myself if they done that. I would have too. (*Matter-of-fact, no self-pity.*)

BENNIE. But they took him away after he was born.

ARLENE. Yeah. (*Bennie waits, knowing she is about to say more.*) An I guess I went crazy after that. Thought if I could jus git out an find him . . .

BENNIE. I don't remember any of that on the TV.

ARLENE. No.

BENNIE. Just remember you smilin at the cameras, yellin how you tol that cab driver not to touch you.

ARLENE. I never seen his cab. (*Now forces herself to begin to eat.*)

ARLIE. (*In the cell, holding a pillow and singing.*) Rock-a-bye baby, on the tree top, when the wind blows, the cradle will . . . (*Not remembering.*) cradle will . . . (*Now talking.*) what you gonna be when you grow up, pretty boy baby? You gonna be a doctor? You gonna give people medicine an take out they . . . no, don't be no doctor . . . be . . . be a preacher . . . sayin Our Father who is in Heaven . . . Heaven, that's where people go when they dies, when doctors can't save em or somebody kills em fore they even git a chance to . . . no, don't be no preacher neither . . . be . . . go to school an learn good (*Tone begins to change.*) so you kin . . . make everbody else feel so stupid all the time. Best thing you to be is stay a baby cause nobody beats up on babies or puts them . . . (*Much more quiet.*) that ain't true, baby. People is mean to babies, so you stay right here with me so nobody kin git you an make you cry an they lay one finger on you (*Hostile.*) an I'll beat the screamin shit right out of em. They even blow on you an I'll kill em. (*Bennie and Arlene have finished their dinner. Bennie puts one carton of slaw in the refrigerator, then picks up all the paper, making a garbage bag out of one of the sacks.*)

BENNIE. Ain't got a can, I guess. Jus use this ol sack for now.

ARLENE. I ain't never emptyin another garbage can.

BENNIE. Yeah, I reckon you know how by now. (*Yawns.*) You bout ready for bed?

ARLENE. (*Stands up.*) I spose.

BENNIE. (*Stretches.*) Little tired myself.

ARLENE. Thanks for the chicken. (*Dusting the crumbs off the bed.*)

36

BENNIE. You're right welcome. You look beat. How bout I rub your back. (*Grabs her shoulders.*)

ARLENE. (*Pulling away.*) No. (*Walking to the sink.*) You go on now.

BENNIE. Oh come on. (*Wiping his hands on his pants.*) I ain't all that tired.

ARLENE. *I'm* tired.

BENNIE. Well, see then, a back rub is just what the doctor ordered.

ARLENE. No. I don't . . . (*Pulling away.*)

BENNIE. (*Grabs her shoulders and turns her around, sits her down hard on the trunk, starts rubbing her back and neck.*) Muscles git real tight like, right in here.

ARLENE. You hurtin me.

BENNIE. Has to hurt a little or it won't do no good.

ARLENE. (*Jumps, he has hurt her.*) Oh, stop it! (*Slips away from him and out into the room. She is frightened.*)

BENNIE. (*Smiling, coming after her, toward the bed.*) Be lot nicer if you was layin down. Wouldn't hurt as much.

ARLENE. Now, I ain't gonna start yellin. I'm jus tellin you to go.

BENNIE. (*Straightens up as though he's going to cooperate.*) O.K. then. I'll jus git my hat. (*He reaches for the hat, then turns quickly, grabs her and throws her down on the bed. He starts rubbing again.*) Now, you just relax. Don't you go bein scared of me.

ARLENE. You ain't gettin nuthin from me.

BENNIE. I don't want nuthin, honey. Jus tryin to help you sleep.

ARLENE. (*Struggling.*) Don't you call me honey.

BENNIE. (*Stops rubbing, but keeps one hand on her back. Rubs her hair with his free hand.*) See? Don't that feel better?

ARLENE. Let me up.

BENNIE. Why, I ain't holdin you down. (*So innocent.*)

ARLENE. Then let me up.

BENNIE. (*Takes hands off.*) O.K. Git up.

ARLENE. (*Turns over slowly, begins to lift herself up on her elbows. Bennie puts one hand on her leg.*) Move your hand.

BENNIE. (*Arlene gets up, moves across the room.*) I'd be happy to stay here with you tonight. Make sure you'll be all right. You ain't spent a night by yourself for a long time.

ARLENE. I remember how.

BENNIE. Well how you gonna git up? You got a alarm?

ARLENE. It ain't all that hard.

37

BENNIE. (*Puts one hand in his pocket, leers a little.*) Oh yeah it is. (*Walks toward her again.*) Gimme a kiss. Then I'll go.

ARLENE. You stay away from me. (*Edging along the counter, seeing she's trapped.*)

BENNIE. (*Reaches for her, clamping her hands behind her, pressing up against her.*) Now what's it going to hurt you to give me a little ol kiss?

ARLENE. Git out! I said git out! (*Struggling.*)

BENNIE. You don't want me to go. You're jus beginning to git interested. Your ol girlie temper's flarin up. I like that in a woman.

ARLENE. Yeah, you'd love it if I'd swat you one. (*Gettin away from him.*)

BENNIE. I been hit by you before. I kin take anything you got.

ARLENE. I could mess you up good.

BENNIE. Now, Arlie. You ain't had a man in a long time. And the ones you had been no count.

ARLENE. Git out! (*Slaps him. He returns the slap.*)

BENNIE. (*Moving in.*) Ain't natural goin without it too long. Young thing like you. Git all shriveled up.

ARLENE. (*Arlie turning on, now.*) All right, you sunuvabitch, you asked for it! (*Goes into a violent rage, hitting and kicking him.*)

BENNIE. (*Overpowering her capably, prison guard style.*) Little outta practice, ain't you? (*Amused.*)

ARLENE. (*Screaming.*) I'll kill you, you creep!

BENNIE. (*Struggle continues, Bennie pinning her arms under his legs as he kneels over her on the bed. Arlene is terrified and in pain.*) You will? You'll kill ol Bennie . . . kill ol Bennie like you done that cab driver? (*A cruel reminder he employs to stun and mock her. Arlene looks as though she has been hit. Bennie is still fired up, he unzips his pants.*)

ARLENE. (*Passive, cold and bitter.*) This how you got your Dorrie, rapin?

BENNIE. (*Unbuttoning his shirt.*) That what you think this is, rape?

ARLENE. I oughta know.

BENNIE. Uh-huh.

ARLENE. First they unzip their pants. (*Bennie pulls his shirt out.*) Sometimes they take off their shirt.

BENNIE. They do huh?

ARLENE. But mostly, they just pull it out and stick it in. (*Bennie*

38

stops, one hand goes to his fly, finally hearing what she has been saying. He straightens up, obviously shocked. He puts his arms back in his shirt.)

BENNIE. Don't you call me no rapist. *(Pause, then insistent.)* No, I ain't no rapist, Arlie. *(Gets up, begins to tuck his shirt back in and zip up his pants.)*

ARLENE. And I ain't Arlie.

BENNIE. *(Arlene remains on the bed as he continues dressing.)* No, I guess you ain't.

ARLENE. *(Quietly and painfully.)* Arlie coulda killed you.

END OF ACT I

OVER LOUDSPEAKER—BEFORE ACT II CURTAIN

These announcements will be heard during the last 5 minutes of the intermission.

Garden workers will, repeat, will, report for work this afternoon. Bring a hat and raincoat and wear boots. All raincoats will be checked at the front gate at the end of work period and returned to you after supper.

Your attention please. A checkerboard was not returned to the recreation area after dinner last night. Anyone with information regarding the black and red checkerboard missing from the recreation area will please contact Mrs. Duvall after lunch. No checkerboards or checkers will be distributed until this board is returned.

Betty Rickey and Mary Alice Wolf report to the laundry. Doris Creech and Arlie Holsclaw report immediately to the superintendent's office. The movie this evening will be "Dirty Harry" starring Clint Eastwood. Doris Creech and Arlie Holsclaw report to the superintendent's office immediately.

The bus from St. Mary's this Sunday will arrive at 1:00 P.M. as usual. Those residents expecting visitors on that bus will gather on the front steps promptly at 1:20 and proceed with the duty officer to the visiting area after it has been confirmed that you have a visitor on the bus.

Attention all residents. Attention all residents. (*Pause.*) Mrs. Helen Carson has taught needlework classes here at Pine Ridge for 30 years. She will be retiring at the end of this month and moving to Florida where her husband has bought a trailer park. The resident council and the Superintendent's staff has decided on a suitable retirement present. We want every resident to participate in this project—which is—a quilt, made from scraps of material collected from the residents and sewn together by residents and staff alike. The procedure will be as follows. A quilting room has been set up in an empty storage area just off the infirmary. Scraps of fabric will be collected as officers do evening count. Those residents who would enjoy cutting up old uniforms and bedding no longer in use should sign up for this detail with your dorm officer. If you would like to sign your name or send Mrs. Carson some special message on your square of fabric, the officers will have tubes of embroidery paint for that purpose. The backing for the quilt has been donated by the Women's Associates as well as the refreshments for the retirement party to be held after lunch on the 30th. Thank you very much for your attention and participation in this worthwhile tribute to someone we are all very fond of here. You may resume work at this time. Doris Creech and Arlie Holsclaw report to the superintendent's office immediately.

ACT II

The next morning. Arlene is asleep on the bed. Arlie is locked in a maximum security cell. We do not see the officer to whom she speaks.

ARLIE. No, I don't have to shut up, neither. You already got me in seg-re-ga-tion, what else you gonna do? I got all day to sleep, while everbody else is out bustin ass in the laundry. (*Laughs.*) Hey! I know . . . you ain't gotta go do no dorm count, I'll just tell you an you jus sit. Huh? You preciate that? Ease them corns you been moanin about . . . yeah . . . O.K. Write this down. (*Pride, mixed with alternating contempt and amusement.*) Startin down by the john on the back side, we got Mary Alice. Sleeps with her pillow stuffed in her mouth. Says her Mom says it'd keep her from grindin down her teeth or somethin. She be suckin that pillow like she gettin paid for it. (*Laughs.*) Next, it's Betty the Frog. Got her legs all opened out like some fuckin . . . (*Makes croaking noises.*) Then it's Doris eatin pork rinds. Thinks somebody gonna grab em outta her mouth if she eats em during the day. Doris ain't dumb. She fat, but she ain't dumb. Hey! You notice how many girls is fat here? Then it be Rhonda, snorin, Marvene, wheezin and Suzanne, coughin. Then Clara an Ellie be still whisperin. Family shit, who's gettin outta line, which girls is gittin a new work 'signment, an who kin git extra desserts an for how much. Them's the two really run this place. My bed right next to Ellie, for sure it's got some of her shit hid in it by now. Crackers or some crap gonna leak out all over my sheets. Last time I found a fuckin grilled cheese in my pillow. Even had two of them little warty pickles. Christ! O.K. Linda and Lucille. They be real quiet, but they ain't sleepin. Prayin, that's them. Linda be sayin them Hell Mary's till you kin just about scream. An Lucille, she tol me once she didn't believe in no God, jus some stupid spirits whooshin aroun everwhere makin people do stuff. Weird. Now, I'm goin back down the other side, there's . . . (*Screams.*) I'd like to see you try it! I been listenin at you for the last three hours. Your husband's gettin laid off an your lettuce is gettin eat by rabbits. Crap City. *You* shut up! Whadda I care if I wake everybody up? I want the nurse . . . I'm gittin sick in here . . . an there's bugs in here! (*The light comes up in the apartment. Faint morning traffic sounds are heard. Arlene does not wake up. The Warden walks across the catwalk. The Guard-Evans catches up with him near Arlie's cell. Bennie is stationed at the far end of the walk.*)

LOUDSPEAKER. Dorm A may now eat lunch.

GUARD-EVANS. Warden, I thought 456 . . . (*Nodding in Arlie's direction.*) was leavin here.

WARDEN. Is there some problem?

GUARD-EVANS. Oh, we can take care of her all right. We're just tired of takin her shit, if you'll pardon the expression.

ARLIE. (*Interrupting.*) You ain't seen nuthin yet, you mother.

WARDEN. Washington will decide on her transfer. Til then, you do your job.

GUARD-EVANS. She don't belong here. Rest of . . .

LOUDSPEAKER. (*Interrupts him.*) Betty Rickey and Mary Alice Wolf report to the laundry.

GUARD-EVANS. Most of these girls are mostly nice people, go along with things. She needs a cage.

ARLIE. (*Vicious.*) I need a knife.

WARDEN. Had it occurred to you that we could send the rest of them home and just keep her? (*Very curt. Walks away.*)

LOUDSPEAKER. Dorm A may now eat lunch. A Dorm to lunch.

GUARD-EVANS. (*Turning around, muttering to himself.*) Oh, that's a swell idea. Let everybody out except bitches like Holsclaw. (*She makes an obscene gesture at him, he turns back toward the catwalk.*) Smartass Warden, thinks he's runnin a hotel.

BENNIE. (*Having overheard this last interchange.*) Give you some trouble, did she?

GUARD-EVANS. I can wait.

BENNIE. For what?

GUARD-EVANS. For the day she tries gettin out an I'm here by myself. I'll show that screachin slut a thing or . . .

BENNIE. That ain't the way, Evans.

GUARD-EVANS. The hell it ain't. Beat the livin . . .

BENNIE. Outta a little thing like her? Gotta do her like all the rest. You got your shorts washed by givin Betty Rickey *Milky Ways.* You git your chairs fixed givin Frankie Hill extra time in the

43

shower with Lucille Smith. An you git ol Arlie girl to behave her-self with a stick of gum. Gotta have her brand, though.

GUARD-EVANS. You screwin that wildcat?

BENNIE. (*Starts walk to Arlie's cell.*) Watch. (*Arlie is silent as he approaches, but is watching intently.*) Now, (*To nobody in particular.*) where was that piece of Juicy Fruit I had in this pocket. Gotta be here somewhere. (*Takes a piece of gum out of his pocket and drops it within Arlie's reach.*) Well, (*Feigning disappointment.*) I guess I already chewed it. (*Arlie reaches for the gum and gets it.*) Oh, (*Looking down at her now.*) how's it goin, kid?

ARLIE. O.K. (*Arlie says nothing, but unwraps the gum and chews it. Bennie leaves the cell area, motioning to the other guard as if to say, "See, that's how it's done." A loud siren goes by in the street below the apartment. Arlene bolts up out of bed, then turns back to it quickly, making it up in a frenzied, ritual manner. As she tucks the spread up under the pillow, the siren stops and so does she. For the first time, now, she looks around the room, realizing where she is and the habit she has just played out. A jackhammer noise gets louder. She walks over to the window and looks out. There is a wolf-whistle from a worker below. She shuts the window in a fury, then grabs the bars. She starts to shake them, but then her hand goes limp. She looks around the room, as if trying to remember what she is doing there. She looks at her watch, now aware that it is late and that she has slept in her clothes.*)

ARLENE. People don't sleep in their clothes, Arlene. An people git up fore noon. (*Arlene makes a still disoriented attempt to pull herself together, changing shoes, combing her hair, washing her face, etc., as guards and other prison life continues on the catwalk.*)

WARDEN. (*Walking up to Arlie, remaining some distance from her, but talking directly to her, as he appears to check files or papers.*) Good afternoon, Arlie.

ARLIE. Fuck you. (*Warden walks away.*) Wait! I wanna talk to you.

WARDEN. I'm listening.

ARLIE. When am I gittin outta here?

WARDEN. That's up to you.

ARLIE. The hell it is.

WARDEN. When you can show that you can be with the other girls, you can get out.

ARLIE. How'm I supposed to prove that bein in here?

WARDEN. And then you can have mail again and visitors.

ARLIE. You're just fuckin with me. You ain't ever gonna let me out. I been in this ad-just-ment room four months, I think.

WARDEN. Arlie, you see the other girls on the dorm walking around, free to do whatever they want? If we felt the way you seem to think we do, everyone would be in lockup. When you get out of segregation, you can go to the records office and have your time explained to you.

ARLIE. It won't make no sense.

WARDEN. They'll go through it all very slowly . . . when you're eligible for parole, how many days of good time you have, how many industrial days you've earned, what constitutes meritorious good time . . . and how many days you're set back for your write-ups and all your time in segregation.

ARLIE. I don't even remember what I done to git this lockup.

WARDEN. Well, I do. And if you ever do it again, or anything like it again, you'll be right back in lockup where you will stay until you forget *how* to do it.

ARLIE. What was it?

WARDEN. You just remember what I said.

ARLENE. Now, then . . . (*Sounds as if she has something in mind to do. Looks as though she doesn't.*)

ARLIE. What was it?

WARDEN. Oh, and Arlie, the prison chaplain will be coming by to visit you today.

ARLIE. I don't want to see no chaplain!

WARDEN. Did I ask you if you wanted to see the chaplain? No, I did not. I said, the chaplain will be coming by to visit you today. Mrs. Roberts, why hasn't this light bulb been replaced? (*To an unseen guard. Walks away.*)

ARLIE. (*Screaming.*) Get out of my hall! (*Warden walks away. Arlene walks to the refrigerator and opens it. She picks out a carton of slaw Bennie put there last night. She walks away from the door, then turns around, remembering to close it. She looks at the slaw, as guard comes up to Arlie's cell with a plate.*)

ARLENE. I ain't never eatin no more scrambled eggs.

GUARD-CALDWELL. Chow time, cutie pie.

ARLIE. These eggs ain't scrambled, they's throwed up! And I want a fork! (*Arlene realizes she has no fork, then fishes one out of the garbage sack from last night. She returns to the bed, takes a bite of slaw and gets her wallet out of her purse. She lays the bills out on the bed one at a time.)*

ARLENE. That's for coffee . . . and that's for milk and bread . . . an that's cookies . . . an cheese an crackers . . . an shampoo an soap . . . an bacon an livercheese. No, pickle loaf . . . an ketchup and some onions . . . an peanut butter an jelly . . . an shoe polish. Well, ain't no need gettin everything all at once. Coffee, milk, ketchup, cookies, cheese, onions, jelly. Coffee, milk . . . oh, shampoo . . .

RUBY. *(Off banging on the door, yelling.)* Candy, I gotta have my five dollars back.

ARLENE. *(Quickly stuffing her money back in her wallet.)* Candy ain't here!

RUBY. It's Ruby, upstairs. She's got five dollars I loaned her . . . Arlie? That Arlie? Candy told me her sister be . . . *(Arlene opens the door hesitantly.)* It is Arlie, right?

ARLENE. It's Arlene. *(Does not extend her hand.)*

RUBY. See, I got these shoes in layaway . . . *(Puts her hand back in her pockets.)* she said you been . . . you just got . . . you seen my money?

ARLENE. No.

RUBY. I don't get em out today they go back on the shelf.

ARLENE. *(Doesn't understand.)* They sell your shoes?

RUBY. Yeah. Welcome back.

ARLENE. Thank you. *(Embarrassed, but relieved.)*

RUBY. She coulda put it in my mailbox. *(Ruby starts to leave, Arlene is closing the door behind her, when Ruby turns around.)* Uh . . . listen . . . if you need a phone, I got one most of the time.

ARLENE. I do have to make this call.

RUBY. Ain't got a book though . . . well, I got one but it's holdin up my bed. *(Laughs.)*

ARLENE. I got the number.

RUBY. Well, then . . . *(Awkward.)*

ARLENE. Would you . . . wanna come in?

RUBY. You sure I'm not interruptin anything?

ARLENE. I'm sposed to call my parole officer.

RUBY. Good girl. Most of them can't talk but you call em anyway. *(Arlene does not laugh.)* Candy go back to that creep?

ARLENE. I guess.

46

RUBY. I's afraid of that. (*Looking around.*) Maybe an envelope with my name on it? Really cleaned out the place, didn't she?
ARLENE. Yeah. Took everything. (*They laugh a little.*)
RUBY. Didn't have much. Didn't do nuthin here 'cept . . . sleep.
ARLENE. Least the rent's paid til the end of the month. I'll be workin by then.
RUBY. You ain't seen Candy in a while.
ARLENE. No. Think she was in the 7th grade when . . .
RUBY. She's growed up now, you know.
ARLENE. Yeah. I was thinkin she might come by.
RUBY. Honey, she won't be comin by. He keeps all his . . . (*Starting over.*) his place is pretty far from here. But . . . (*Stops, trying to decide what to say.*)
ARLENE. But what?
RUBY. But she had a lot of friends, you know. *They* might be comin by.
ARLENE. Men, you mean.
RUBY. Yeah. (*Quietly, waiting for Arlene's reaction.*)
ARLENE. (*Realizing the truth.*) Mother said he was her boyfriend.
RUBY. I shouldn't have said nuthin. I jus didn't want you to be surprised if some john showed up, his tongue hangin out an all. (*Sits down on the bed.*)
ARLENE. It's O.K. I shoulda known anyway. (*Now suddenly angry.*) No, it ain't O.K. Guys got their dirty fingernails all over her. Some pimp's out buyin green pants while she . . . Goddamn her.
RUBY. Hey now, that ain't your problem. (*Moves toward her, Arlene backs away.*)
ARLIE. (*Pointing.*) You stick your hand in here again Doris an I'll bite it off.
RUBY. She'll figure it out soon enough.
ARLIE. (*Pointing to another person.*) An you, you ain't my Mama, so you can cut the Mama crap.
ARLENE. I wasn't gonna cuss no more.
RUBY. Nuthin in the parole rules says you can't git pissed. My first day outta Gilbertsville I done the damn craziest . . . (*Arlene looks around, surprised to hear Ruby has done time.*) Oh yeah, a long time ago, but . . . hell, I heaved a whole gallon of milk right out the window my first day.
ARLENE. (*Somewhat cheered.*) It hit anybody?

RUBY. It bounced! Make me feel a helluva lot better. I said, "Ruby, if a gallon of milk can bounce back, so kin you."

ARLENE. That's really what you thought?

RUBY. Well, not exactly. I had to keep sayin it for bout a year fore I finally believed it. I's moppin this lady's floor once an she come in an heard me sayin "gallon-a'-milk, gallon-a'-milk," fired me. She did. Thought I was too crazy to mop her floors. (*Laughs, but is still bitter. Arlene wasn't listening. Ruby wants to change the subject now.*) Hey! You have a good trip? Candy said you was in Arkansas.

ARLENE. Alabama. It was O.K. This guard, well he used to be a guard, he just quit. He ain't never seen Kentucky, so he drove me. (*Watching for Ruby's response.*)

RUBY. Pine Ridge?

ARLENE. Yeah.

RUBY. It's co-ed now, ain't it?

ARLENE. Yeah. That's dumb, you know. They put you with men so's they can git you if you're seen with em.

RUBY. Sposed to be more natural, I guess.

ARLENE. I guess.

RUBY. Well, I say it sucks. Still a prison. No matter how many pictures they stick up on the walls or how many dirty movies they show, you still gotta be counted 5 times a day. (*Now beginning to worry about Arlene's silence.*) You don't seem like Candy said.

ARLENE. She tell you I was a killer?

RUBY. More like the meanest bitch that ever walked. I seen lots worse than you.

ARLENE. I been lots worse.

RUBY. Got to you, didn't it? (*Arlene doesn't respond, but Ruby knows she's right.*) Well, you jus gotta git over it. Bein out, you gotta . . .

ARLENE. Don't you start in on me.

RUBY. (*Realizing her tone.*) Right, sorry.

ARLENE. It's O.K.

RUBY. Ex-cons is the worst. I'm sorry.

ARLENE. It's O.K.

RUBY. Done that about a year ago. New waitress we had. Gave my little goin straight speech, "No booze, no men, no buyin on credit," shit like that, she quit that very night. Stole my fuckin raincoat on her way out. Some speech, huh? (*Laughs, no longer resenting this theft.*)

ARLENE. You a waitress?

RUBY. I am the Queen of Grease. Make the finest french fries you ever did see.

ARLENE. You make a lot of money?

RUBY. I sure know how to. But I ain't about to go back inside for doin it. Cookin out's better'n eatin in, I say.

ARLENE. You think up all these things you say?

RUBY. Know what I hate? Makin salads—cuttin up all that stuff 'n floppin it in a bowl. Some day . . . some day . . . I'm gonna hear "tossed salad" an I'm gonna do jus that. Toss out a tomato, toss out a head a' lettuce, toss out a big ol carrot. (*Miming the throwing act and enjoying herself immensely.*)

ARLENE. (*Laughing.*) Be funny seein all that stuff flyin outta the kitchen.

RUBY. Hey Arlene! (*Gives her a friendly pat.*) You had your lunch yet?

ARLENE. (*Pulling away immediately.*) I ain't hungry.

RUBY. (*Carefully.*) I got raisin toast.

ARLENE. No. (*Goes over to the sink, twists knobs as if to stop a leak.*)

ARLIE. Whaddaya mean, what did she do to me? You got eyes or is they broke? You only seein what you feel like seein. I git ready to protect myself from a bunch of weirdos an then you look.

ARLENE. Sink's stopped up. (*Begins to work on it.*)

ARLIE. You ain't seein when they's leavin packs of cigarettes on my bed an then thinking I owe em or somethin.

RUBY. Stopped up, huh? (*Squashing a bug on the floor.*)

ARLIE. You ain't lookin when them kitchen workers lets up their mommies in line nights they know they only baked half enough brownies.

RUBY. Let me try.

ARLIE. You ain't seen all the letters comin in an goin out with visitors. I'll tell you somethin. One of them workmen buries dope for Betty Rickey in little plastic bottles under them sticker bushes at the water tower. You see that? No, you only seein me. Well, you don't see shit.

RUBY. (*A quiet attempt.*) Gotta git you some Drano if you're gonna stay here.

ARLIE. I'll tell you what she done. Doris brung me some rollers from the beauty school class. 3 fuckin pink rollers. Them plastic ones with the little holes. I didn't ask her. She jus done it.

RUBY. Let me give her a try.

ARLENE. I can fix my own sink.

ARLIE. I's stupid. I's thinkin maybe she were different from all them others. Then that night everbody disappears from the john and she's wantin to brush my hair. Sure, brush my hair. How'd I know she was gonna crack her head open on the sink? I jus barely even touched her.

RUBY. (*Walking to the bed now, digging through her purse.*) Want a Chiclet?

ARLIE. You ain't asked what she was gonna do to me. Huh? When you gonna ask that? You don't give a shit about that cause Doris such a good girl.

ARLENE. Don't work. (*Giving up.*)

RUBY. We got a dishwasher quittin this week if you're interested.

ARLENE. I need somethin that pays good.

RUBY. You type?

ARLENE. No.

RUBY. Do any clerk work?

ARLENE. No.

RUBY. Any key punch?

ARLENE. No.

RUBY. Well, then I hate to tell you, but all us old-timers already got all the good cookin and cleanin jobs. (*Smashes another bug, goes to the cabinet to look for the bug spray.*) She even took the can of Raid! Just as well, empty anyway. (*Arlene doesn't respond.*) She hit the bugs with it. (*Still no response.*) Now, there's that phone call you was talkin about.

ARLENE. Yeah.

RUBY. (*Walking toward the door.*) An I'll git you that number for the dishwashin job, just in case. (*Arlene backs off.*) How bout cards? You play any cards? Course you do. I get sick of beatin myself all the time at solitaire. Damn borin bein so good at it.

ARLENE. (*Goes for her purse.*) Maybe I'll jus walk to the corner an make my call from there.

RUBY. It's always broke.

ARLENE. What?

50

RUBY. The phone . . . at the corner. Only it ain't at the corner. It's inside the A & P.

ARLENE. Maybe it'll be fixed.

RUBY. Look, I ain't gonna force you to play cards with me. It's time for my programs anyway.

ARLENE. I gotta git some pickle loaf an . . . things.

RUBY. Suit yourself. I'll be there if you change your mind.

ARLENE. I have some things I gotta do here first.

RUBY. (*Trying to leave on a friendly basis.*) Look, I'll charge you a dime if it'll make you feel better.

ARLENE. (*Takes her seriously.*) O.K.

RUBY. (*Laughs, then realizes Arlene is serious.*) Mine's the one with the little picture of Johnny Cash on the door. (*Walks to the door and leaves. Bennie's singing begins almost immediately, as Arlene walks toward the closet. She is delaying going to the store, but is determined to go. She checks little things in the room, remembers to get a scarf, changes shoes, checks her wallet, finally, as she is walking out, she stops and looks at the picture of Jesus, then moves closer, having noticed a dirty spot. She goes back into the bathroom for a tissue, wets it in her mouth, then dabs at the offending spot. She puts the tissue in her purse then leaves the room when noted.*)

BENNIE. (*To the tune of "I'll Toe The Line," walks across the catwalk carrying a tray with cups and a pitcher of water.*) I keep my pants up with a piece of twine. I keep my eyes wide open all the time, Da da da da-da da da da da da (*Doesn't know this line.*) If you'll be mine, please pull the twine.

ARLIE. You can't sing for shit.

BENNIE. (*Starts down the stairs toward Arlie's cell.*) You know what elephants got between their toes?

ARLIE. I don't care.

BENNIE. Slow natives. (*Laughs.*)

ARLIE. That ain't funny.

GUARD-EVANS. (*As Bennie opens Arlie's door.*) Hey, Davis.

BENNIE. Conversation is rehabilitatin, Evans. Want some water?

ARLIE. O.K.

BENNIE. How bout some Kool-Aid tᴏ go in it? (*Gives her a glass of water.*)

ARLIE. When does the chaplain come?

BENNIE. Want some gum?

ARLIE. Is it today?

BENNIE. *Kool-Aid's* gone up, you know. 15¢ and tax. You get out, you'll learn all about that.

ARLIE. Does the chaplain come today?

BENNIE. (*Going back up the catwalk.*) Income tax, sales tax, property tax, gas and electric, water, rent . . .

ARLIE. Hey!

BENNIE. Yeah, he's comin, so don't mess up.

ARLIE. I ain't.

BENNIE. What's he tell you anyway, get you so starry-eyed?

ARLIE. He jus talks to me.

BENNIE. I talk to you.

ARLIE. Where's Frankie Hill?

BENNIE. Gone.

ARLIE. Out?

BENNIE. Pretty soon.

ARLIE. When.

BENNIE. Miss her don't you? Ain't got nobody to bullshit with. Stories you gals tell . . . whoo-ee!

ARLIE. Get to cut that grass now, Frankie, honey.

BENNIE. Huh?

ARLIE. Stupidest thing she said. (*Gently.*) Said first thing she was gonna do when she got out . . . (*Arlene leaves the apartment.*)

BENNIE. Get laid.

ARLIE. Shut up. First thing was gonna be going to the garage. Said it always smelled like car grease an turpur . . . somethin.

BENNIE. Turpentine.

ARLIE. Yeah, an gasoline, wet. An she'll bend down an squirt oil in the lawnmower, red can with a long pointy spout. Then cut the grass in the back yard, up an back, up an back. They got this grass catcher on it. Says she likes scoopin up that cut grass an spreadin it out under the trees. Says it makes her real hungry for some lunch. (*A quiet curiosity about all this.*)

BENNIE. I got a power mower, myself.

ARLIE. They done somethin to her. Took out her nerves or somethin. She . . .

BENNIE. She jus got better, that's all.

ARLIE. Hah. Know what else? They give her a fork to eat with last week. A fork. A fuckin fork. Now how long's it been since I had a fork to eat with?

BENNIE. (*Getting ready to leave the cell.*) Wish I could help you with that, honey.

ARLIE. (*Loud.*) Don't call me honey.

BENNIE. (*Locks the door behind him.*) That's my girl.

ARLIE. I ain't your girl.

BENNIE. (*On his way back up the stairs.*) Screechin wildcat.

ARLIE. What time is it? (*Very quiet. Arlene walks back into the apartment. She is out of breath and has some trouble getting the door open. She is carrying a big sack of groceries. As she sets the bag on the counter, it breaks open, spilling cans and packages all over the floor. She just stands and looks at the mess. She takes off her scarf and sets down her purse, still looking at the spilled groceries. Finally, she bends down and picks up the package of pickle loaf. She starts to put it on the counter, then turns suddenly and throws it at the door. She stares at it as it falls.*)

ARLENE. Bounce? (*In disgust.*) Shit. (*Arlene sinks to the floor. She tears open the package of pickle loaf and eats a piece of it, tearing off the bites in her mouth. She is still angry, but is completely unable to do anything about her anger.*)

ARLIE. Who's out there? Is anybody out there? (*Reading.*) Depart from evil and do good. (*Yelling.*) Now, you pay attention out there cause this is right out of the Lord's mouth. (*Reading.*) And dwell, that means live, dwell for-ever-more. (*Speaking.*) That's like for longer than I've been in here or longer than . . . this Bible the chaplain give me's got my name right in the front of it. Hey! Somebody's sposed to be out there watchin me. Wanna hear some more? (*Reading.*) For the Lord for . . . (*The word is forsaketh.*) I can't read in here, you turn on my light, you hear me? Or let me out and I'll go read it in the TV room. Please let me out. I won't scream or nuthin. I'll just go right to sleep, O.K.? Somebody! I'll go right to sleep. O.K.? You won't even know I'm there. Hey! Goddammit, somebody let me out of here, I can't stand it in here any more. Somebody! (*Her spirit finally broken.*)

ARLENE. (*She draws her knees up, wraps her arms around them and rests her head on her arms.*) Jus gotta git a job an make some money an everything will be all right. You hear me, Arlene? You git yourself up an go find a job. (*Continues to sit.*) An you kin start by cleanin up this mess you made cause food don't belong on the floor. (*Still sitting. Carl appears in the doorway of the*

53

apartment. When he sees Arlene on the floor, he goes into a fit of vicious, sadistic laughter.)

CARL. What's happenin, Mama? You havin lunch with the bugs?

ARLENE. *(Quietly.)* Fuck off.

CARL. *(Threatening.)* What'd you say?

ARLENE. *(Reconsidering.)* Go away.

CARL. You watch your mouth or I'll close it up for you.

ARLENE. *(Stands up now. Carl goes to the window and looks out, as if checking for someone.)* They after you, ain't they? *(Carl sniffs, scratches at his arm.)*

CARL. *(Finding a plastic bag near the bed, stuffed with brightly colored knitted things. He pulls out baby sweaters, booties and caps.)* What the fuck is this?

ARLENE. You leave them be.

CARL. You got a baby hid here somewhere? I foun its little shoes. *(Laughs, dangling them in front of him.)*

ARLENE. Them's mine. *(Chasing him.)*

CARL. Aw sugar, I ain't botherin nuthin. Just lookin. *(Pulls more out of the sack, dropping one or two on the floor, kicking them away with his feet.)*

ARLENE. *(Picking up what he's dropped.)* I ain't tellin you again. Give me them.

CARL. *(Turns around quickly, walking away with a few of the sweaters.)* How much these go for?

ARLENE. I don't know yet.

CARL. I'll jus take care of em for you—a few coin for the trip. You *are* gonna have to pay your share, you know.

ARLENE. You give me them. I ain't goin with you. *(She walks toward him.)*

CARL. You ain't? *(Mocking, Arlene walks up close to him now, taking the bag in her hands. He knocks her away and onto the bed.)* Straighten up, girlie. *(Now kneels over her.)* You done forgot how to behave yourself. *(Moves as if to threaten her, but kisses her on the forehead, then moves out into the room.)*

ARLENE. *(Sitting up.)* I worked hard on them things. They's nice, too, for babies and little kids.

CARL. I bet you fooled them officers good, doin this shit. *(Throws the bag in the sink.)*

ARLENE. I weren't . . .

CARL. *(Interrupting.)* I kin see that scene. They sayin . . . *(Puts* on a high Southern voice.) "I'd jus love one a' them nice yella sweaters."

ARLENE. They liked them.

CARL. Those turkeys, sure they did. Where else you gonna git your free sweaters an free washin an free step-right-up-git-your-convict-special-shoe-shine. No, don't give me no money, officer. I's jus doin this cause I likes you. (Uncle Tom talk.)

ARLENE. They give em for Christmas presents.

CARL. (Checks the window again, then peers into the grocery sack.) What you got sweet, Mama? (Pulls out a box of cookies and begins to eat them.)

ARLIE. I'm sweepin, Doris, cause it's like a pigpen in here. So you might like it, but I don't, so if you get some mops, I'll take one of them, too.

ARLENE. You caught another habit, didn't you?

CARL. You turned into a narc or what?

ARLENE. You scratchin an sniffin like crazy.

CARL. I see a man eatin cookies an that's what you see too.

ARLENE. An you was laughin at me sittin on the floor! You got cops lookin for you an you ain't scored yet this morning. You better git yourself back to prison where you can git all you need.

CARL. Since when Carl couldn't find it if he really wanted it?

ARLENE. An I bought them cookies for me.

CARL. An I wouldn't come no closer if I's you.

ARLENE. (Stops, then walks to the door.) Then take the cookies an git out.

CARL. (Imitating Bennie.) Oh, please, Miss Arlene, come go with Carl to the big city. We'll jus have us the best time.

ARLENE. I'm gonna stay here an git a job an save up money so's I kin git Joey. (Opening the door.) Now, I ain't sposed to see no ex-cons.

CARL. (Big laugh.) You don't know nobody else. Huh, Arlie? Who you know ain't a "con-vict"?

ARLENE. I'll meet em.

CARL. And what if they don't wanna meet you? You ain't exactly a nice girl, you know. An you gotta be jivin about that job shit. (Throws the sack of cookies on the floor.)

ARLENE. I kin work. (Retrieving the cookies.)

CARL. Doin what?

ARLENE. I don't know. Cookin, cleanin, somethin that pays good.

55

CARL. You got your choice, honey. You can do cookin an cleanin OR you can do somethin that pays good. You ain't gonna git rich working on your knees. You come with me an you'll have money. You stay here, you won't have shit.

ARLENE. Ruby works an she does O.K.

CARL. You got any *Kool-Aid*? (*Looking in the cabinets, moving Arlene out of his way.*) Ruby who?

ARLENE. Upstairs. She cooks. Works nights an has all day to do jus what she wants.

CARL. And what, exactly, do she do? See flicks take rides in cabs to pick up see-through shoes?

ARLENE. She watches TV, plays cards, you know.

CARL. Yeah, I know. Sounds just like the dayroom in the fuckin joint.

ARLENE. She likes it.

CARL. (*Exasperated.*) All right. Say you stay here an *finally* find yourself some job. (*Grabs the picture of Jesus off the wall.*) This your boyfriend?

ARLENE. The chaplain give it to me.

CARL. Say it's dishwashin, O.K.? (*Arlene doesn't answer.*) O.K.?

ARLENE. O.K. (*Takes the picture, hangs it back up.*)

CARL. An you git maybe 75 a week. 75 for standin over a sink full of greasy gray water, fishin out blobs of bread an lettuce. People puttin pieces of chewed up meat in their napkins and you gotta pick it out. 8 hours a day, 6 days a week, to make 75 lousy pictures of Big Daddy George. Now, how long it'll take you to make 75 workin for me?

ARLENE. A night. (*Sits on the bed, Carl pacing in front of her.*)

CARL. Less than a night. Two hours maybe. Now, it's the same fuckin 75 bills. You can either work all week for it or make it in 2 hours. You work two hours a night for me an how much you got in a week? (*Arlene looks puzzled by the multiplication required. Carl sits down beside her, even more disgusted.*) Two 75's is 150. Three 150's is 450. You stay here you git 75-a week. You come with me an you git 450 a week. Now, 450, Arlie, is *more* than 75. You stay here you gotta work 8 hours a day and your hands git wrinkled and your feet swell up (*Suddenly distracted.*) There was this guy at Bricktown had webby toes like a duck. (*Back now.*) You come home with me you work 2 hours a night an you kin sleep all mornin an spend the day buyin eyelashes an tryin out

56

perfume. Come home, have some guy openin the door for you sayin, "Good Evenin, Miss Holsclaw, nice night now ain't it? (*Puts his arm around her.*)

ARLENE. It's Joey I'm thinkin about.

CARL. If you was a kid, would you want your Mom to git so dragged out washin dishes she don't have no time for you an no money to spend on you? You come with me, you kin send him big orange bears an *Sting-Ray* bikes with his name wrote on the fenders. He'll like that. Holsclaw. (*Amused.*) Kinda sounds like coleslaw, don't it? Joey be tellin all his friends bout his Mom livin up in New York City an bein so rich an sendin him stuff all the time.

ARLENE. I want to be with him.

CARL. (*Now stretches out on the bed, his head in her lap.*) So, fly him up to see you. Take him on that boat they got goes roun the island. Take him up to the Empire State Building, let him play King Kong. (*Rubs her hair, unstudied tenderness.*) He be talkin bout that trip his whole life.

ARLENE. (*Smoothing his hair.*) I don't want to go back to prison, Carl.

CARL. (*Jumps up, moves toward the refrigerator.*) There any chocolate milk? (*Distracted again.*) You know they got this motel down in Mexico named after me? Carlsbad Cabins. (*Proudly.*) Who said anything about goin back to prison? (*Slams the refrigerator door, really hostile.*) What do you think I'm gonna be doin? Keepin you out, that's what!

ARLENE. (*Stands up.*) Like last time? Like you gettin drunk? Like you lookin for kid junkies to beat up?

CARL. God, ain't it hot in this dump. You gonna come or not? You wanna wash dishes, I could give a shit. (*Now yelling.*) But you comin with me, you say it right now, lady! (*Grabs her by the arm.*) Huh?

RUBY. (*Knocks on the door.*) Arlene?

CARL. She ain't here! (*Yelling.*)

RUBY. (*Alarmed.*) Arlene! You all right?

ARLENE. That's Ruby I was tellin you about.

CARL. (*Catches her arm again, very rough.*) We ain't through!

RUBY. (*Opening the door.*) Hey! (*Seeing the rough treatment.*) Goin to the store. (*Very firm.*) Thought maybe you forgot somethin.

CARL. (*Turns Arlene loose.*) You this cook I been hearin about?

RUBY. I cook. So what?

CARL. Buys you nice shoes, don't it, cookin? Why don't you hock your watch an have somethin done to your hair? If you got a watch.

RUBY. Why don't you drop by the coffee shop. I'll spit in your eggs.

CARL. They let you bring home the half-eat chili dogs?

RUBY. You . . . you got half-eat chili dogs for brains. (*To Arlene.*) I'll stop by later. (*Contemptuous look for Carl.*)

ARLENE. No. Stay. (*Carl gets the message.*)

CARL. (*Goes over to the sink to get a drink of water out of the faucet, then looks down at his watch.*) Piece a' shit. (*Thumps it with his finger.*) Shoulda took the dude's hat, jack. Guy preachin about the end of the world ain't gonna own a watch that works.

ARLENE. (*Walks over to the sink, bends over Carl.*) You don't need me. I'm gittin too old for it, anyway.

CARL. I don't discuss my business with strangers in the room. (*Heads for the door.*)

ARLENE. When you leavin?

CARL. Six. You wanna come, meet me at this bar. (*Gives her a brightly colored matchbook.*) I'm havin my wheels delivered. (*With faintly uncertain pride.*)

ARLENE. You stealin a car?

CARL. Take a cab. (*Gives her a dollar.*) You don't come . . . well, I already laid it out for you. I ain't never lied to you, have I girl?

ARLENE. No.

CARL. Then you be there. That's all the words I got. (*Makes an unconscious move toward her.*) I don't beg nobody. (*Backs off.*) Be there. (*Turns abruptly and leaves. Arlene watches him go, folding up the money in the matchbook. The door remains open.*)

ARLIE. (*Reading, or trying to, from a small testament.*) For the Lord forsaketh not his Saints, but the seed of the wicked shall be cut off.

RUBY. (*Walks over to the counter, starts to pick up some of the groceries lying on the floor, then stops.*) I 'magine you'll want to be puttin these up yourself. (*Arlene continues to stare out the door.*) He do this?

ARLENE. No.

58

RUBY. Can't trust these sacks. I seen bag boys punchin holes in em at the store.

ARLENE. Can't trust anybody. (*Finally turning around.*)

RUBY. Well, you don't want to trust him, that's for sure.

ARLENE. We spent a lot of time together, me an Carl.

RUBY. He live here?

ARLENE. No, he jus broke outta Bricktown near where I was. I got word there sayin he'd meet me. I didn't believe it then, but he don't lie, Carl don't.

RUBY. You thinkin of goin with him?

ARLENE. They'll catch him. I told him but he don't listen.

RUBY. Funny ain't it, the number a' men come without ears.

ARLENE. How much that dishwashin job pay?

RUBY. I don't know. Maybe 75.

ARLENE. That's what he said.

RUBY. He tell you you was gonna wear out your hands and knees grubbin for nuthin, git old an be broke an never have a nice dress to wear? (*Sitting down.*)

ARLENE. Yeah.

RUBY. He tell you nobody's gonna wanna be with you cause you done time?

ARLENE. Yeah.

RUBY. He tell you your kid gonna be ashamed of you an nobody's gonna believe you if you tell em you changed?

ARLENE. Yeah.

RUBY. Then he was right. (*Pauses.*) But when you make your two nickels, you can keep both of em.

ARLENE. (*Shattered by these words.*) Well, I can't do that.

RUBY. Can't do what?

ARLENE. Live like that. Be like bein dead.

RUBY. You kin always call in sick . . . stay home, send out for pizza an watch your Johnny Carson on TV . . . or git a bus way out Preston Street an go bowlin . . .

ARLENE. (*Anger building.*) What am I gonna do? I can't git no work that will pay good cause I can't do nuthin. It'll be years fore I have a nice rug for this place. I'll never even have some ol Ford to drive around, I'll never take Joey to no fair. I won't be invited home for pot roast and I'll have to wear this fuckin dress for the rest of my life. What kind of life is that?

RUBY. It's outside.

59

ARLENE. Outside? Honey I'll either be *inside* this apartment or *inside* some kitchen sweatin over the sink. Outside's where you get to do what you want, not where you gotta do some shit job jus so's you can eat worse than you did in prison. That ain't why I quit bein so hateful, so I could come back and rot in some slum.
RUBY. (*Word "slum" hits hard.*) Well, you can wash dishes to pay the rent on your "slum," or you can spread your legs for any shit that's got the ten dollars. (*With obvious contempt.*)
ARLENE. (*Not hostile.*) An I don't need you agitatin me.
RUBY. An I don't live in no slum.
ARLENE. (*Sensing Ruby's hurt.*) Well, I'm sorry . . . it's just . . . I thought . . . (*Increasingly upset.*)
RUBY. (*Finishing her sentence to her.*) . . . it was gonna be different. Well, it ain't. And the sooner you believe it, the better off you'll be. (*A guard enters Arlie's cell.*)
ARLIE. Where's the chaplain? I got somethin to tell him.
ARLENE. They said I's . . .
GUARD-CALDWELL. He ain't comin.
ARLENE. . . . he tol me if . . . I thought once Arlie . . .
ARLIE. It's Tuesday. He comes to see me on Tuesday.
GUARD-CALDWELL. Chaplain's been transferred, dollie. Gone. Bye-bye. You know.
ARLENE. He said the meek, meek, them that's quiet and good . . . the meek . . . as soon as Arlie . . .
RUBY. What, Arlene? Who said what?
ARLIE. He's not comin back?
ARLENE. At Pine Ridge there was . . .
ARLIE. He woulda told me if he couldn't come back.
ARLENE. I was . . .
GUARD-CALDWELL. He left this for you.
ARLENE. I was . . .
GUARD-CALDWELL. Picture of Jesus, looks like.
ARLENE. . . . this chaplain . . .
RUBY. Arlene . . . (*Trying to call her back from this hysteria.*)
ARLIE. (*Hysterical.*) I need to talk to him.
ARLENE. This chaplain . . .
ARLIE. You tell him to come back and see me.
ARLENE. I was in lockup . . .
ARLIE. (*A final, anguished plea.*) I want the chaplain!
ARLENE. I don't know . . . years . . .

RUBY. And . . .

ARLENE. This chaplain said I had . . . said Arlie was my hateful self and she was hurtin me and God would find some way to take her away . . . and it was God's will so I could be the meek . . . the meek, them that's quiet and good an git whatever they want . . . I forgit that word . . . they git the Earth.

RUBY. Inherit.

ARLENE. Yeah. And that's why I done it.

RUBY. Done what?

ARLENE. What I done. Cause the chaplain he said . . . I'd sit up nights waitin for him to come talk to me.

RUBY. Arlene, what did you do? What are you talkin about?

ARLENE. They tol me . . . after I's out an it was all over . . . they said after the chaplain got transferred . . . I didn't know why he didn't come no more til after . . . they said it was three whole nights at first, me screamin to God to come git Arlie an kill her. They give me this medicine an thought I's better . . . then that night it happened, the officer was in the dorm doin count . . . an they didn't hear nuthin but they come back out where I was an I'm standin there tellin em to come see, real quiet I'm tellin em, but there's all this blood all over my shirt an I got this fork I'm holdin real tight in my hand . . . (*Clenches one hand now, the other hand fumbling with the buttons as if she's going to show Ruby.*) this fork, they said Doris stole it from the kitchen an give it to me so I'd kill myself and shut up botherin her . . . an there's all these holes all over me where I been stabbin myself an I'm sayin Arlie is dead for what she done to me, Arlie is dead an it's God's will . . . I didn't scream it, I was jus sayin it over and over . . . Arlie is dead, Arlie is dead . . . they couldn't git that fork outta my hand til . . . I woke up in the infirmary an they said I almost died. They said they's glad I didn't. (*Smiling.*) They said did I feel better now an they was real nice, bringing me chocolate puddin . . .

RUBY. I'm sorry, Arlene. (*Reaches out for her, but Arlene pulls away sharply.*)

ARLENE. I'd be eatin or jus lookin at the ceiling an git a tear in my eye, but it'd jus dry up, you know, it didn't run out or nuthin. An then pretty soon, I's well, an officers was sayin they's seein such a change in me an givin me yarn to knit sweaters an how'd I like to have a new skirt to wear an sometimes lettin me chew gum.

They said things ain't never been as clean as when I's doin the housekeepin at the dorm. (*So proud.*) An then I got in the honor cottage an nobody was foolin with me no more or nuthin. An I didn't git mad like before or nuthin. I jus done my work an knit . . . an I don't think about it what happened, cept . . . (*Now losing control.*) people here keep callin me Arlie an . . . (*Has trouble saying "Arlie."*) I didn't mean to do it, what I done . . .

RUBY. Oh, honey . . . (*Trying to help.*)

ARLENE. I did . . . (*This is very difficult.*) I mean, Arlie was a pretty mean kid, but I did . . . (*Very quickly.*) I didn't know what I . . . (*Breaks down completely, screaming, crying, falling over into Ruby's lap.*) Arlie! (*Grieving for this lost self.*)

RUBY. (*Rubs her back, her hair, waiting for the calm she knows will come. Finally, but very quietly.*) You can still . . . (*Now obviously referring to some personal loss of her own.*) . . . you can still love people that's gone. (*Ruby continues to hold her tenderly, rocking as with a baby. A terrible crash is heard on the steps outside the apartment.*)

BENNIE'S VOICE. Well, chicken pluckin, hog kickin shit!

RUBY. Don't you move now, it's just somebody out in the hall.

ARLENE. That's . . .

RUBY. It's O.K., Arlene. Everything's gonna be just fine. Nice and quiet now.

ARLENE. That's Bennie that guard I told you about.

RUBY. I'll get it. You stay still now. (*She walks to the door, and looks out into the hall, hands on hips.*) Why you dumpin them flowers on the stairs like that? Won't git no sun at all! (*Turns back to Arlene.*) Arlene, there's a man plantin a garden out in the hall. You think we should call the police or get him a waterin' can?

BENNIE. (*Appearing in the doorway, carrying a box of dead looking plants.*) I didn't try to fall, you know.

RUBY. Well, when you git ready to try, I wanna watch! (*Blocking the door.*)

ARLENE. I thought you's gone.

RUBY. (*To Bennie.*) You got a visitin pass?

BENNIE. (*Coming into the room.*) Arlie . . . (*Quickly.*) Arlene. I brung you some plants. You know, plants for your window. Like we talked about, so's you don't see them bars.

RUBY. (*Picking up one of the plants.*) They sure is scraggly lookin things. Next time, git plastic.

BENNIE. I'm sorry I dropped em, Arlene. We kin get em back together an they'll do real good. (*Setting them down on the trunk.*) These ones don't take the sun. I asked just to make sure. Arlene?

RUBY. You up for seein this petunia killer?

ARLENE. It's O.K. Bennie, this is Ruby, upstairs.

BENNIE. (*Bringing one flower over to show Arlene, stuffing it back into its pot.*) See? It ain't dead.

RUBY. Poor little plant. It comes from a broken home.

BENNIE. (*Walks over to the window, getting the box and holding it up to the window.*) That's gonna look real pretty. Cheerful-like.

RUBY. Arlene ain't gettin the picture yet. (*Walking to the window and holding her plant up, too, posing.*) Now. (*Arlene looks, but is not amused.*)

BENNIE. (*Putting the plants back down.*) I jus thought, after what I done last night . . . I jus wanted to do somethin nice.

ARLENE. (*Calmer now.*) They is nice. Thanks.

RUBY. Arlene says you're a guard.

BENNIE. I was. I quit. Retired.

ARLENE. Bennie's goin back to Alabama.

BENNIE. Well, I ain't leavin right away. There's this guy at the motel says the bass is hittin pretty good right now. Thought I might fish some first.

ARLENE. Then he's goin back.

BENNIE. (*To Ruby as he washes his hands.*) I'm real fond of this little girl. I ain't goin til I'm sure she's gonna do O.K. Thought I might help some.

RUBY. Arlene's had about all the help she can stand.

BENNIE. I got a car, Arlene. An money. An . . . (*Reaching into his pocket.*) I brung you some gum.

ARLENE. That's real nice, too. An I 'preciate what you done, bringin me here an all, but . . .

BENNIE. Well, look. Least you can take my number at the motel an give me a ring if you need somethin. (*Gives her a piece of paper.*) Here, I wrote it down for you. (*Arlene takes the paper.*) Oh, an somethin else, these towel things . . . (*Reaching into his pocket, pulling out the packaged towelettes.*) they was in the chicken last night. I thought I might be needin em, but they give us new towels every day at that motel.

ARLENE. O.K. then. I got your number.

BENNIE. (*Backing up toward the door.*) Right. Right. Any ol

63

thing, now. Jus any ol thing. You even run outta gum an you call.

RUBY. Careful goin down.

ARLENE. Bye Bennie.

BENNIE. Right. The number now. Don't lose it. You know, in case you need somethin.

ARLENE. No. (*Bennie leaves, Arlene gets up and picks up the matchbook Carl gave her and holds it with Bennie's piece of paper.*)

RUBY. (*Watches a moment, sees Arlene trying to make this decision, knowing that what she says now is very important.*) We had this waitress put her phone number in matchbooks, give em to guys left her nice tips. Anyway, one night this little ol guy calls her and comes over and says he works at this museum an he don't have any money but he's got this hat belonged to Queen Victoria. An she felt real sorry for him so she screwed him for this little ol lacy hat. Then she takes the hat back the next day to the museum thinkin she'll git a reward or somethin an you know what they done? (*Pause.*) Give her a free membership. Tellin her thanks so much an we're so grateful an wouldn't she like to see this mummy they got downstairs . . . an all the time jus stallin . . . waiting cause they called the police.

ARLENE. You do any time for that?

RUBY. (*Admitting the story was about her.*) County jail.

ARLENE. (*Quietly, looking at the matchbook.*) County jail. (*Arlene tears up the matchbook and drops it in the sack of trash.*) You got any *Old Maids?*

RUBY. Huh?

ARLENE. You know.

RUBY. Cards? (*Surprised and pleased.*)

ARLENE. (*Laughs a little.*) It's the only one I know.

RUBY. Old Maid, huh? (*Not her favorite game.*)

ARLENE. I gotta put my food up first.

RUBY. Bout an hour?

ARLENE. I'll come up.

RUBY. Great. (*Stopping by the plants on her way to the door.*) These plants is real ugly. (*Fondly. Exits. Arlene watches her, then turns back to the groceries still on the floor. Slowly, but with great determination, she picks up the items one at a time and puts them away in the cabinet above the counter. Arlie appears on the catwalk, one light on each of them.*)

ARLIE. Hey! You member that time we was playin policeman an June locked me up in Mama's closet an then took off swimmin? An I stood around with them dresses itchin my ears an crashin into that door tryin to git outta there? It was dark in there. So, finally, (*Very proud.*) I went around an peed in all Mama's shoes. But then she come home an tried to git in the closet only June taken the key so she said, "Who's in there?" an I said, "It's me!" and she said, "What you doin in there?" an I started gigglin an she started pullin on the door an yellin, "Arlie, what you doin in there?" (*Big laugh.*)

ARLIE and ARLENE. (*Arlene has begun to smile during the story, now they say together, both standing as Mama did, one hand on her hip.*) Arlie, what you doin in there?

ARLENE. (*Still smiling and remembering, stage dark except for one light on her face.*) Aw shoot. (*Light dims on her fond smile as Arlie laughs once more.*)

THE END

GETTING OUT

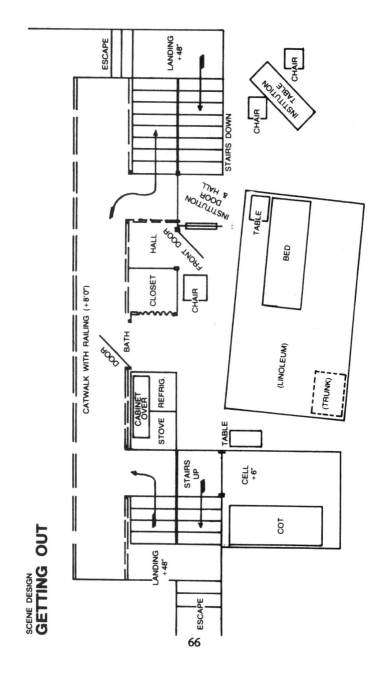

FURNITURE PROPS

1 Porcelain Toilet—white, seat, no-seat cover
1 Combination Sink/Refrigerator Unit
   approx. 30"H, 24"W, 48"L
   Sink is practical and has swan neck faucet, to facilitate
   filling bucket
1 Gas Oven w/Burners—*Not Practical*
2 White Metal Cabinets—on wall over sink & stove
1 Studio Bed—single
   Box Spring on 6" wood legs
   Mattress attached to box spring > bed is made during perf.
   (This unit must be *very, very* sturdy)
1 Metal Prison/Army Type Cot w/Headboard but *no* Footboard
   or rail above mattress height.
   (Bare metal springs are jumped & sat on
   must be re-inforced with hemp webbing)
1 Straw-filled Mattress for Cot w/Plastic Mattress Bag
1 Small White Metal Table—3 shelves
   approx. 30"H, 18"W, 24"L
2 Plain Metal & Wood Chairs—matching
1 Metal Table approx. 30"H, 18"W, 48"L
1 Small Parsons Table—Plastic
1 Side Chair (May Be Bentwood) (very sturdy)
   is kicked cross-stage each perf.
1 Spare Side Chair
   Old Newspapers (Kentucky, Alabama . . .)
1 Large Trunk approx. 18"H, 24"W, 36"L. Flat Top
   w/Removable Tray Handles on Each End of Trunk
   Trunk & Tray must be very sturdy
1 Small Honey Jar—Empty
2 Brooms—Straw
2 Cardboard Boxes approx 24" square
1 Tin Foil Ashtray (Sm. *Morton* Pie Tin)
1 Empty Coke Can (For misc. trash in boxes)
2 Bottles of "Big Red" (1 spare)
4 Wire Coat Hangers
1 Wire Coat Hanger w/Top Untwisted
1 Box of Book Matches

11 One Dollar Bills
1 Black Leather Doctor's Bag
3 Large Key Rings with keys
3 Leather Belt Thongs (For Key Rings)
1 Grey Wool Army Blanket
4 Black Disposable Lighters (for toilet)
1 Box of small wooden kitchen matches
2 Vinyl Two Fold Clipboards 1)Brown 1)Black
2 Identical Framed Pictures of Jesus approx. 14"✕17"
1 U-Shaped White Curtain Rod w/Fasteners
2 Black Purses (1 Mother—1 Ruby)
2 Black Wallets (Men's) (1 Arlene—1 Mother)
  Red spray paint (To make spot on floor)
2 Syringes w/Dull Needles (1 spare)
1 Large Plastic Clothes Basket—Rectangular
1 Box of Medical Alcohol Swabs
1 Orange Plastic Bead Necklace (Elastic String)
1 Crashbox—Sounds like dropping wood box of potted plants
1 Bright Red Matchbook w/Printing
  (1 matchbook Torn up for each perf.)
1 Plastic "Wonder Bread Bag"
  In Bag: Plastic Knitted Baby Clothes
    Yellow Knitted Baby Booties
1 Set Cafe Curtains—Faded Pastel Print
1 Small Copper Tea Pot w/Red Wood Handle
  Heavyweight Paper Plates—Plain White
  Plastic or Styrofoam Food Boxes
1 Faded Pink Chenille Bedspread—Single
1 Faded Floral Print Fitted Bottom Sheet—Single
1 Flat Top Sheet—Single
1 White Fitted Bottom Sheet ⎫
1 White Flat Top Sheet   ⎬ For Cot
                              ⎭
2 White Pillow Cases (1 for bed—1 for cot)
2 Old Single Feather Pillows—Striped
1 Small Box of *Tampax*
1 Small Motel Soap
4 Pink Plastic Hair Rollers
4 Plastic, Metal Bracelets—Bright Colors—easy to slip on
1 Woman's Hair Brush
1 Roll of Toilet Paper
1 Small Package of Steel Wool Pads
1 Wooden Pot Scrub Brush
1 Floor Scrub Brush

2 Brightly Colored Sponges
2 Small Rags
2 White Dish Towels
1 Can Insect Spray
2 Small Soft Plastic Tumblers
1 Can Ajax
1 Can floor wax
1 Plastic Bottle *Mr. Clean*
1 Package of Paper Towels
1 Box *Brillo*
1 *Tuffy*
1 *Handi-Wipe* package
1 Sm. Package of Garbage Bags
1 Hand Towel ⎫
1 Face Towel ⎬ Different Colors
1 Bath Towel—Aged White ⎭
2 Identical Yellow Plastic Buckets
1 Large Paper Grocery Bag Plain—Per Show
  Note: Unglue Bottom and Re-Fold—Used As Breakaway
1 1 lb. Paper package of coffee—A & P
1 Qt. Carton of Milk—Empty, filled w/Clay for weight
1 Box of *Oreo* Cookies—Opened Each Perf.
  approx. 5 cookies eaten each perf.
1 Fake Package of Pickle Loaf Lunch Meat
1 Plastic Net Bag of Onions—fake
1 Plastic Shoe Polish Bottle—empty—filled for weight
1 Plastic Shampoo Bottle—fake but weighted
1 Non-Breakable Jar of Jelly
1 Non-Breakable Jar of Peanut Butter
5 Manilla Letter Size File Folders
  Assorted Form-Like Type Papers (Medical, Prison Records, etc.)
1 Small Plastic Ashtray—Slightly Damaged
1 Empty Potato Chip Bag
1 Empty ConDom Wrapper (ConDom used as trash on floor top of
  show)
1 Empty Box of Crackers
1 Package of Cloth-Covered Rubber Bands—For Hair
1 Pack *Juicy Fruit* Gum (unopened)
  Sticks of Sugarless Gum in *Juicy Fruit* Wrappers
1 Straight Razor—Tape Edge—(Carl)
1 Lg. Bucket of *Kentucky Fried Chicken*
  Note: Gets Thrown on the Floor Each Perf.
    Top taped so it won't open when thrown on floor

1   *Kentucky Fried* Paper Bag
    In Bag: Full 2 Cans Coke
             2 Paper Napkins
             2 Containers Cole Slaw } per show
             2 Plastic Forks
1   Shallow Wooden Box approx. 3"H, 15"W, 24"L
6–10 Small Potted Plants—To Fit in Box
1   Box of Wash & Dri Type Towelettes
1   Cardboard Take-Out Coffee Cup—Per Show
1   Package of *Chicklets*—2 Eaten Per Show
1   Small Bible w/Ribbon Marker
1   Apple—Per Show
1   *PlayBoy* Magazine
1   *True Confessions* Magazine
1   White Enameled Metal Pitcher
1   Package of Small (4 oz.) Paper Cups
2   Cafeteria Type Trays—Brown
1   Pr. Metal-Framed Glasses (Doctor)
1   Old Stuffed Teddy Bear
1   Small Tube of Tooth Paste
1   Small Package of Kool-Aid—Per Show
1   Small Piece of Paper w/Phone numbers
4   Men's Wristwatches
2   Women's Wristwatches
1   Cane

ACT I — PRESHOW PRESET

Sweep & mop floors—especially cell
Trunk outside front door—preset
Replace both door breakaways
Latch on front door retracted
Rotten apple in refrigerator
Light switch—up position
Bathroom door SLIGHTLY ajar
Hook up sink and check water runs
Empty drain bucket for sink
Extra yellow bucket in bathroom (w/water)
Touch up linoleum floor with brown paint (if needed)
Cell bed against bars R.
Metal table & chairs on spike L.
Check nail in wall
Toilet in cell
Lighter taped in toilet
White metal cabinet by U. edge of cell plat
Bentwood chair overturned—R. of front door
Check red paint spots
Matches on white metal cabinet (small kitchen matches)
Cell door open
2 Girlie magazines by head of bed D. side on floor.
Paper on floor—one piece nightstand under (U. of head of bed)
Window open 3"
D.S. Section of curtain open
Mattress on cell bed
Blanket on foot of cell bed—special fold (to open quickly)
Pillow on each bed
Hanger in closet—on R. side (made easy to take apart)
Arlene's purse—D.S. of cell bed (ON FLOOR)
    cigarettes, matches, compact, lipstick, wallet
    w/10 dollars, 3 pieces of toilet paper,
    gum
Scarf—on Arlene's purse
Trash in cabinet over sink (2 boxes)
Section of paper S.L. of sink on floor
2 Cardboard boxes U.S. end of white metal cabinet on floor
3 Torn pictures in top cardboard box

71

Yellow ashtray in top cardboard box
Pot-pie plate top shelf white metal cabinet
Tray with plate, scrambled eggs, roll—on cell bed
Honey jar—top shelf white metal cabinet
S.L. PROP
Dr. vinyl folder
Warden's clipboard
Dr.'s cane
BREAK-AWAY-BAG
Grocery bag—with Oreo's, shampoo, shoe polish, pickle loaf,
    bread, onion's, crackers, peanut butter, jelly, milk
Coffee cup with water in it
Stick of gum
Arlie's hat
OUTSIDE FRONT DOOR
Crash box
Mother's broom
Laundry basket—loaded
Trunk—Bennie's hat on trunk
S.R. PROP
Dr. bag—syringe and towelettes inside
Bible
Picture of Jesus
Plate of food (covered)
Box of food—fake (weighted)
Broom
Arlie's potato chips
Stick of gum (sugarless)
S.C. PROP
Tray with 5 glasses—pitcher—packet of Kool-Aid
Bucket of chicken
Sack with 2 cokes, 2 forks, 2 cole slaw, 2 napkins
1 Dollar—(Carl)
1 Matchbook—(Carl)
1 Big Red bottle—small amount of red liquid in bottle—(Carl)
Box of flowers—with towelettes, paper, gum (Bennie)

ACT II—INTERMISSION

Check trunk spike
Light switch—up position
Hairbrush on top of metal cabinet
Slot in padded cell door—open
Bed sheet (apt. bed) turned down U. side

Cole slaw in refrigerator
Check curtains closed
Fork on top of chicken bucket
Hairband D. edge of metal cabinet by brush top shelf
Arlene's scarf—2nd shelf white metal cabinet
Bible at head of cell bed—bindings facing D.
Toilet out of cell
Padding around cell (5 sections plus door unit)
Check wire hanger in closet (should be on R. side of closet)
Arlene's shoes at foot of bed—heel face away from bed
Arlene's purse on nightstand—money folded over
Wallet (wallet hooked over front purse pocket)
Cell door closed
Cigs on metal shelf-top
Bathroom door ajar
Remove cardboard box by head of bed
Check furniture spikes esp. cell bed
Joey Bear—U. head of bed
Remove Bennie's hat to backstage
Remove Big Red bottle
Put away cleaning supplies from mother scene
Remove coke cans from nightstand
Close L. door (next to L. stairs)
Strike bedding from cell bed
Check Arlene's 2nd act dress, make sure it is easily accessible
Check sink, make sure water is running and faucet is running into sink
Put bentwood chair against wall R. of front door
Straighten Jesus picture
Check front door breakaways—pick up any pieces on floor, place under bed.
Check padded door openings—make sure they are easily operable

NEW PLAYS

★ **BRIGHT HALF LIFE by Tanya Barfield.** A moving love story that spans decades in an instant—from marriage, children, skydiving, and the infinite moments that make a life together. "BRIGHT HALF LIFE, a sixty-five minute chronicle of a deeply committed lesbian relationship, is contemporary as a play could be but the theme is classic and timeless… the presentation of the highs and lows of coupledom, as exampled in this piece, defy the ages." *–Huffington Post.* [2W] ISBN: 978-0-8222-3351-0

★ **WAIT UNTIL DARK by Frederick Knott, adapted by Jeffrey Hatcher.** Forty-seven years after *Wait Until Dark* premiered on Broadway, Jeffrey Hatcher has adapted Frederick Knott's 1966 original, giving it a new setting. In 1944 Greenwich Village, Susan Hendrix, a blind yet capable woman, is imperiled by a trio of men in her own apartment. As the climax builds, Susan discovers that her blindness just might be the key to her escape, but she and her tormentors must wait until dark to play out this classic thriller's chilling conclusion. "… reminds CGI-infected audiences that a few shadows, a shiny knife, and compelling characters can still go a long way to create suspense… WAIT UNTIL DARK earns its climax through enthralling, layered characters." *–Entertainment Weekly.* [4M, 2W] ISBN: 978-0-8222-3205-6

★ **BAKERSFIELD MIST by Stephen Sachs.** Maude, a fifty-something un-employed bartender living in a trailer park, has bought a painting for a few bucks from a thrift store. Despite almost trashing it, she's now convinced it's a lost masterpiece by Jackson Pollock worth millions. But when world-class art expert Lionel Percy flies over from New York and arrives at her trailer home in Bakersfield to authenticate the painting, he has no idea what he is about to discover. Inspired by true events, this hilarious and thought-provoking new comedy-drama asks vital questions about what makes art and people truly authentic. "A triumph! Hugely gratifying! An absorbing, hilarious two-hander about the nature of art and the vagaries of human perception." *–Backstage.* "Sachs' short, clever play is a battle of wits." *–NY Times.* [1M, 1W] ISBN: 978-0-8222-3280-3

★ **SWITZERLAND by Joanna Murray-Smith.** Somewhere in the Swiss Alps, grande dame of crime literature Patricia Highsmith lives with an impressive collection of books, and a somewhat sinister collection of guns and knives. She finds solace in her solitude, her cats, and cigarettes. But when a mysterious international visitor arrives at her perfectly secluded home, her love of fictional murders becomes a dangerous reality. "[SWITZERLAND] explores what it's like to be a woman writer in a man's literary kingdom… Murray-Smith's dialogue sparkles with witty one-liners and delicious snark…" *–Time Out (Sydney).* [1M, 1W] ISBN: 978-0-8222-3435-7

DRAMATISTS PLAY SERVICE, INC.
440 Park Avenue South, New York, NY 10016 212-683-8960
postmaster@dramatists.com www.dramatists.com

NEW PLAYS

★ **EMERGING ARTIST GRANT by Angus MacLachlan.** Ethan, a successful independent filmmaker, is sweating over casting his newest project in his hometown of Winston-Salem when Spencer, a newly-minted adjunct theatre professor, auditions for the lead. Their mutual attraction is immediate, and they start a charming and amusing dance of personal and professional eroticism. Ethan's smart and witty older sister, Liz, is thrown into the mix. She supports herself as a hairdresser; her acting career, and her hopes, have derailed a bit with time. A subtly comedic story set in the creative world, EMERGING ARTIST GRANT explores how we struggle to make something of our lives, and it questions the moral crises we encounter when trying for our dreams. "… [A] witty play [and] something of a master class in artistic self-appraisal and survival… the questions of how many interpersonal boundaries are transgressed… remain up in the air until the end." –*IndyWeek.com.* [1M, 2W] ISBN: 978-0-8222-3365-7

★ **THE BELLE OF AMHERST by William Luce.** In her Amherst, Massachusetts, home, the reclusive nineteenth-century poet Emily Dickinson recollects her past through her work, her diaries and letters, and a few encounters with significant people in her life. "William Luce has chiseled a perfectly detailed cameo… He has made an Emily so warm, human, loving and lovable that her ultimate vulnerability will break your heart." –*Boston Globe.* [1W] ISBN: 978-0-8222-3373-2

★ **LET ME DOWN EASY by Anna Deavere Smith.** In this solo show constructed from verbatim interview transcripts, Anna Deavere Smith examines the miracle of human resilience through the lens of the national debate on health care. After collecting interviews with over 300 people on three continents, Smith creates an indelible gallery of 20 individuals, known and unknown—from a rodeo bull rider and a World Heavyweight boxing champion to a New Orleans doctor during Hurricane Katrina, as well as former Texas Governor Ann Richards, cyclist Lance Armstrong, film critic Joel Siegel, and supermodel Lauren Hutton. A work of emotional brilliance and political substance from one of the treasures of the American theater. Originally created as a one-person show, the author encourages multi-actor productions of the play. "It's stunning, beautiful, and transcendent." –*SF Weekly.* [1W] ISBN: 978-0-8222-2948-3

★ **PORT AUTHORITY by Conor McPherson.** PORT AUTHORITY follows three generations of Irishmen as they tell the stories of their lives. "Overwhelmingly poignant…McPherson rivetingly shows how the past is in all our presents." –Evening Standard (London). "McPherson occupies his familiar terrain with glittering wit and assurance… he writes like a recording Irish angel…[with] a poetic understanding of what might have been." –*Guardian (UK).* [3M] ISBN: 978-0-8222-3311-4

DRAMATISTS PLAY SERVICE, INC.
440 Park Avenue South, New York, NY 10016 212-683-8960
postmaster@dramatists.com www.dramatists.com

NEW PLAYS

★ **BETWEEN RIVERSIDE AND CRAZY by Stephen Adly Guirgis. Winner of the 2015 Pulitzer Prize.** Ex-cop and recent widower Walter "Pops" Washington and his newly paroled son Junior have spent a lifetime living between Riverside and crazy. But now, the NYPD is demanding his signature to close an outstanding lawsuit, the landlord wants him out, the liquor store is closed—and the church won't leave him alone. When the struggle to keep one of New York City's last great rent-stabilized apartments collides with old wounds, sketchy new houseguests, and a final ultimatum, it seems that the old days may be dead and gone. "Everyone's bound to be captivated by Guirgis's loudmouthed locals… [and] warm, rich dialect that comes right off the city streets." *–Variety.* [4M, 3W] ISBN: 978-0-8222-3340-4

★ **THE VEIL by Conor McPherson.** May 1822, rural Ireland. The defrocked Reverend Berkeley arrives at the crumbling former glory of Mount Prospect House to accompany a young woman to England. Seventeen-year-old Hannah is to be married off to a marquis in order to resolve the debts of her mother's estate. However, compelled by the strange voices that haunt his beautiful young charge and a fascination with the psychic current that pervades the house, Berkeley proposes a séance, the consequences of which are catastrophic. "… an effective mixture of dark comedy and suspense." *–Telegraph (London).* "A cracking fireside tale of haunting and decay." *–Times (London).* [3M, 5W] ISBN: 978-0-8222-3313-8

★ **ASHVILLE by Lucy Thurber.** Chronologically the second play in Lucy Thurber's The Hill Town Plays cycle, ASHVILLE is the story of Celia, sixteen years old and trapped in her poor white rural town, among people who can't hope for anything more than a good blue-collar job and a decent marriage. Celia wants something else in life, even if she can't articulate what that is. For a fleeting moment she thinks she finds the unnameable thing in her neighbor and tentative friend Amanda, but it may be that no one else can save Celia—only she herself can orchestrate her escape. "The best thing about these five plays is the detailed and quite devastating portrait they present of the depressed industrial region of western Massachusetts…" *–Variety.* [4M, 3W] ISBN: 978-0-8222-3355-8

★ **DOV AND ALI by Anna Ziegler.** Once upon a time, in the middle of a school, in the middle of Detroit, in the middle of the United States of America, there was a confused teacher and a precocious student. When Dov, an orthodox Jew, and Ali, a strict Muslim, get caught in a cultural crossfire, both are confronted with the same choice: Will they stand by their beliefs or face the devastating consequences? "… a flawless play… In a time of ceaseless snark and cynicism, its earnestness in asking bigger questions can be downright refreshing." *–NY Times.* "… an intense, intelligent and hugely promising play…" *–Guardian (UK).* [2M, 2W] ISBN: 978-0-8222-3455-5

DRAMATISTS PLAY SERVICE, INC.
440 Park Avenue South, New York, NY 10016 212-683-8960
postmaster@dramatists.com www.dramatists.com

NEW PLAYS

★ **BUZZER by Tracey Scott Wilson.** Jackson, an upwardly-mobile black attorney, has just bought an apartment in a transitioning neighborhood in Brooklyn. He sees the potential of his old neighborhood, as does his white girlfriend Suzy... at first. When Jackson's childhood friend Don leaves rehab to crash with them, the trio quickly becomes trapped between the tensions inside their own home and the dangers that may lurk outside. "Skillful... [a] slow-burning, thought-provoking drama..." *–NY Times.* "[In BUZZER,] race is not a national conversation but an inner turmoil... the fact that the main gentrifier here is black turns the usual view of the subject inside out: Can one gentrify one's own home?" *–New York Magazine.* [3M, 1W] ISBN: 978-0-8222-3411-1

★ **THE NANCE by Douglas Carter Beane.** In the 1930s, burlesque impresarios welcomed the hilarious comics and musical parodies of vaudeville to their decidedly lowbrow niche. A headliner called "the nance"—usually played by a straight man—was a stereotypically camp homosexual and master of comic double entendre. THE NANCE recreates the naughty, raucous world of burlesque's heyday and tells the backstage story of Chauncey Miles and his fellow performers. At a time when it was easy to play gay and dangerous to be gay, Chauncey's uproarious antics on the stage stand out in marked contrast to his offstage life. "A nearly perfect work of dramatic art..." *–The New Yorker.* [4M, 4W] ISBN: 978-0-8222-3077-9

★ **EMPANADA LOCA by Aaron Mark.** Now living deep under Manhattan in an abandoned subway tunnel with the Mole People, a very hungry Dolores recounts her years selling weed with her boyfriend, her return to Washington Heights after thirteen years in prison, her fortuitous reunion with an old stoner friend who lets her give massages for cash in the basement under his empanada shop, and the bloodbath that sent her fleeing underground. Loosely inspired by the legend of Sweeney Todd, EMPANADA LOCA is contemporary Grand Guignol horror in the style of Spalding Gray. "Exuberantly macabre..." *–NY Times.* "Spine-tingling and stomach-churning..." *–Time Out (NY).* [1W] ISBN: 978-0-8222-3476-0

★ **SENSE OF AN ENDING by Ken Urban.** Charles, a discredited *New York Times* journalist, arrives in Rwanda for an exclusive interview with two Hutu nuns. Charged with alleged war crimes committed during the 1994 genocide, the nuns must convince the world of their innocence or face a lifetime in prison. When an unknown Tutsi survivor contradicts their story, Charles must choose which version of the truth to tell. Based on real events, SENSE OF AN ENDING shines a light on questions of guilt, complicity, and faith in the face of extreme violence. "A superb play... so intense that, in between each scene, you can hear the audience gulp for air." *–Time Out (London).* [3M, 2W] ISBN: 978-0-8222-3094-6

DRAMATISTS PLAY SERVICE, INC.
440 Park Avenue South, New York, NY 10016 212-683-8960
postmaster@dramatists.com www.dramatists.com

NEW PLAYS

★ **PLACEBO by Melissa James Gibson.** A minty green pill—medication or sugar? Louise is working on a placebo-controlled study of a new female arousal drug. As her work in the lab navigates the blurry lines between perception and deception, the same questions pertain more and more to her life at home. With uncanny insight and unparalleled wit, Melissa James Gibson's affectionate comedy examines slippery truths and the power of crossed fingers. "Smart, droll, beautifully observed…" –*New York Magazine.* "… subtle yet intellectually explosive…" –*TheaterMania.com.* [2M, 2W] ISBN: 978-0-8222-3369-5

★ **THE ROAD TO DAMASCUS by Tom Dulack.** As full-scale civil war rages in Syria, a bomb explodes in Manhattan and all roads lead to Damascus. A peace-seeking African Pope is elected to the Vatican and an Evangelical third-party president is in power in the U.S. With nuclear war looming, will the new Pope intervene directly in American foreign policy, or will he accede to the demands of Washington? Riddled with international intrigue, Tom Dulack's astonishingly prescient play imagines a world ripped from today's headlines. "Serious… satisfying… This near-future tale of an ill-conceived American plan feels authentic enough to have you believe that such events could take place any day. Or to remind you that similar ones have already occurred." –*NY Times.* [5M, 2W] ISBN: 978-0-8222-3407-4

★ **FOUR PLACES by Joel Drake Johnson.** When Peggy's two adult children take her out for lunch, they quietly begin to take apart her life. The drinks come fast, the tempers peak, the food flies. "… a meticulously structured work that captures a decades-long history of paralyzing family resentments, depleted affections, and sublimated cruelties in a single, uninterrupted 90-minute scene." –*Chicago Reader.* "FOUR PLACES is intense, remorseless drama at its finest." –*Backstage.* [1M, 3W] ISBN: 978-0-8222-3448-7

★ **THE BIRDS by Conor McPherson, from a story by Daphne du Maurier.** The short story that inspired Alfred Hitchcock's classic film is boldly adapted by Conor McPherson—a gripping, unsettling, and moving look at human relationships in the face of societal collapse. In an isolated house, strangers Nat and Diane take shelter from relentless masses of attacking birds. They find relative sanctuary but not comfort or peace; there's no electricity, little food, and a nearby neighbor may still be alive and watching them. Another refugee, the young and attractive Julia, arrives with some news of the outside world, but her presence also brings discord. Their survival becomes even more doubtful when paranoia takes hold of the makeshift fortress—an internal threat to match that of the birds outside. "Deliciously chilling… spring-loaded with tension…" –*Irish Independent.* "[McPherson] keeps us on the edge of our seat." –*Irish Times.* [2M, 2W] ISBN: 978-0-8222-3312-1

DRAMATISTS PLAY SERVICE, INC.
440 Park Avenue South, New York, NY 10016 212-683-8960
postmaster@dramatists.com www.dramatists.com

NEW PLAYS

★ **A DELICATE SHIP by Anna Ziegler.** A haunting love triangle triggers an unexpected chain of events in this poetic play. In the early stages of a new relationship, Sarah and Sam are lovers happily discovering each other. Sarah and Nate know everything about each other, best of friends since childhood and maybe something more. But when Nate shows up unannounced on Sarah's doorstep, she's left questioning what and who she wants in this humorous and heartbreaking look at love, memory, and the decisions that alter the course of our lives. "Ziegler (who makes origami of time)… digs beneath the laughs, of which there are plenty, to plumb the pain that lurks below." –*Time Out (NY)*. [2M, 1W] ISBN: 978-0-8222-3453-1

★ **HAND TO GOD by Robert Askins.** After the death of his father, meek Jason finds an outlet for his anxiety at the Christian Puppet Ministry, in the devoutly religious, relatively quiet small town of Cypress, Texas. Jason's complicated relationships with the town pastor, the school bully, the girl next door, and—most especially—his mother are thrown into upheaval when Jason's puppet, Tyrone, takes on a shocking and dangerously irreverent personality all its own. HAND TO GOD explores the startlingly fragile nature of faith, morality, and the ties that bind us. "HAND TO GOD is so ridiculously raunchy, irreverent and funny it's bound to leave you sore from laughing. Ah, hurts so good." –*NY Daily News*. [3M, 2W] ISBN: 978-0-8222-3292-6

★ **PLATONOV by Anton Chekhov, translated by John Christopher Jones.** PLATONOV is Chekhov's first play, and it went unproduced during his lifetime. Finding himself on a downward spiral fueled by lust and alcohol, Platonov proudly adopts as his motto "speak ill of everything." A shining example of the chaos that reigned in his era, Platonov is a Hamlet whose father was never murdered, a Don Juan who cheats on his wife and his mistress, and the hero of the as-yet unwritten great Russian novel of his day. [9M, 4W] ISBN: 978-0-8222-3343-5

★ **JUDY by Max Posner.** It's the winter of 2040, and the world has changed—but maybe not by much. Timothy's wife has just left him, and he isn't taking it well. His sisters, Tara and Kris, are trying to help him cope while wrestling with their own lives and loves. The three of them seem to spend a lot of time in their basements, and the kids are starting to ask questions. This subterranean comedy explores how one family hangs on when technology fails and communication breaks down. "This smart, disturbing comedy is set…just far enough in the future to be intriguingly weird but close enough to the present to be distressingly familiar… Posner's revelations about this brave new world… waver between the explicit and the mysterious, and each scene… gives us something funny and scary to ponder." –*The New Yorker*. [3M, 3W] ISBN: 978-0-8222-3462-3

DRAMATISTS PLAY SERVICE, INC.
440 Park Avenue South, New York, NY 10016 212-683-8960
postmaster@dramatists.com www.dramatists.com